From Grace a Child of God

Ena J. Williams

DENVER, COLORADO

The opinions expressed in this manuscript are solely the opinions of the author and do not represent the opinions or thoughts of the publisher. The author has represented and warranted full ownership and/or legal right to publish all the materials in this book.

From Grace a Child of God
All Rights Reserved.
Copyright © 2013 Ena J. Williams
v2.0

Scripture taken from the HOLY BIBLE, NEW INTERNATIONAL VERSION. Copy 1973, 1978, 1984. International Bible Society. Used by Permission of Zondervan Publishing House.

This story is based on actual events. All names and locations have been changed to protect the privacy of those involved.

This book may not be reproduced, transmitted, or stored in whole or in part by any means, including graphic, electronic, or mechanical without the express written consent of the publisher except in the case of brief quotations embodied in critical articles and reviews.

Outskirts Press, Inc.
http://www.outskirtspress.com

ISBN: 978-1-4787-0651-9

Outskirts Press and the "OP" logo are trademarks belonging to Outskirts Press, Inc.

PRINTED IN THE UNITED STATES OF AMERICA

Acknowledgements

First I would like to thank God; the original caregiver of mankind for all things. To my family who supported me through my years of growth, tears, pain, and sorrow many thanks. To my children and personal caregivers; Ricky Jr., Dominique, Noelle, Kimiko, Ronald, Alana, and Dianne; thank you for the love and compassion which you display daily; without your efforts, patience, time and willingness to work together when it comes to caring for Ricky and I, none of this would have been possible. Lonny and Ronald C. thanks for always taking time out for Ricky, Bryan thanks for being one of the crew. Ricky III, Derick, Sedrick, Rico, and Xavier; thank you for allowing me to be the best Grandma I can be, Xavier you will grow up to be one of the greatest caregivers of all times. Ron P, thank you for God's greatest gift; Dominique and Ronald II; Stacey you really bring out the best in Ron. Charlotte, you too will always be my sister. Rachel and Aprell; thanks for all of your help, without knowing you allowed me time to write. To my Springhill family; thank you for sharing your personal time with me and my family; your prayers are felt, and looking at Ricky and I you can see they are also answered. Special thanks to my friends, and true sisters, Elizabeth and Cynara; you shared my laughter and tears with me through my years, loving and protective when needed, yet always honest even critical when necessary never judging, I love you. To Pastor Ronald G. Arthur; my Pastor, my teacher, my friend and brother; the countless hours of lessons, counsel, guidance, and support to me and my family is immeasurable in this life. Thank you for helping me find my spiritual path, and your constant encouragement to keep that path. To my husband Ricky, thank you for choosing to love me as only you can, you are my best everything; and you bring out the best in me; you are my greatest inspiration, I love you with all that I am, and all that I am to be.

Foreword

Grace. God's grace. God's amazing grace. That saved a wretch like me! And what is God's grace? And how does it save? And whom does it save? And for what does it save?

God's grace is a key attribute of His character that is almost always associated with mercy, love, compassion, and patience. It is supremely and superbly revealed and given in the person and work of Jesus Christ. It is favor or kindness shown without regard to the worth or merit of one who receives and in spite of what that person deserves.

Grace is God's deliverance from danger and destruction that is available to all who avail themselves to it. Grace apprehended and comprehended makes the recipient at once both the beneficiary of God's Grace and the embodiment of God's grace.

God as Spirit conveys His grace through human recipients of His grace, that is, His children.

In my thirty seven years of ministering the gospel, thirty of which have been spent in the pastorate, I have seen no more magnificent paradigm of being both a beneficiary of God's grace and the embodiment of God's grace than in my parishioner Ena Williams. From her life flows grace to others as a child of God.

Diagnosed with Multiple Sclerosis in two thousand and three on her thirty-ninth birthday, she soon became too disabled to work away from home. Her husband Ricky developed Alzheimer's at age fifty-three in 2008 as a result of an aneurysm in the brain. His condition resulted in him being declared medically disabled and unable to continue working. Thus, both were denied working to retirement and reduced to living on disability income.

However, God's grace apprehended, comprehended, and applied to every situation in their lives has led to a peace and prosperity that surpasses all human understanding. Their mutual love and care for each other has not let her succumb to being house or wheel-chair bound, and him to live beyond a three year life expectancy as diagnosed by treating physicians. They are the visible form of marital vows requiring, "for better or worse; in sickness and in health; for richer or for poorer" and thus a marital model for those in our congregation married or contemplating such.

Moreover, Ena has served as the church's bookkeeper initially on site and subsequently from home since contracting her illness.

Furthermore, they have taken in their daughter and her son, and have helped her rear him from birth to Kindergarten.

As if any of the afore-mentioned were not manifestation enough of grace under fire, she serves this Pastor in the dual capacity of spiritual sounding board (saving his sanity repeatedly) and as a surrogate sister to him who lost his sister to breast cancer that eventually spread to her brain in the year two thousand at the age of thirty-seven.

Grace. God's grace. God's amazing grace. That saved a wretch like me! And what is God's grace? It is a grateful child of God, who has received much grace from a child of God named Ena, who hopes this work of grace, will bring much grace, into the lives of many others in need of God's grace.

Ronald Garfield Arthur
Pastor
Springhill Baptist Church
Farmington Hills, Michigan

Table of Contents

Introduction i

Chapter 1:   My Dad 1
Chapter 2:   Grace 6
Chapter 3:   What Is Dementia? 18
Chapter 4:   What's Wrong with Me? 34
Chapter 5:   Expect the Unexpected 46
Chapter 6:   Not My Job! 59
Chapter 7:   I Give Up 73
Chapter 8:   Dreaded Phone Calls 79
Chapter 9:   What Is Hospice? 90
Chapter 10: Divided We Will Fall 100
Chapter 11: Fight Time 110
Chapter 12: Time to Say Goodbye 120
Chapter 13: After Goodbye 133
Chapter 14: Never Ending New Beginnings 141

Epilogue 151

Introduction

AS A CHILD the world is full of endless innocence. Growing up is an adventure in itself.

God provides us with strength unknown and endless. I thank God for loving me in spite of myself. I pray that God continue to bless me and my family with the wisdom and knowledge necessary to stay in his word and continue his work.

> Heavenly Father
> Thank you for being such a good God
> May the meditations of my heart
> And the words of my mouth
> Be acceptable in your sight
> O Lord, my strength
> And my redeemer
> I love you Lord
> Amen

I have many wonderful memories of growing up. I sometimes wonder if it was really my life or was it some story book. Growing up in a large family left nothing to desire; except more bathroom time. My parents definitely provided me with all the love and support that any child could possibly want.

I am one of many branches on God's vine; however my knowledge of this did not come to me early in life. God had a whole lot of pruning to do with me. Although I'm not there yet, I ask God to allow me to get there before I leave here.

"Therefore do not worry about tomorrow, for tomorrow will worry about itself. Each day has enough trouble of its own." (Matthew 6:34)

CHAPTER 1

My Dad

MOST MEN OF today have no idea what a dad is. Sure, all men are capable of being a father, but to be a dad is a whole different dimension. My dad has always been the financial provider for my family, yet he also had a very nurturing quality about himself. He taught me to be strong and to stand up for what I believe is right. He gave me all the necessary ingredients to live a productive life. Pray, trust, listen, obey.

Even when I was disciplined he would recite the commandments to me. After telling me it was for my own good; which I never believed he also never let the day end without making up by giving me a treat. Daddy said, never go to bed angry. It's just not healthy. My father came from a small family, grew up in a small town. He said he always wanted a lot of children because he spent a lot of time alone. Being the eighth of ten children I guess he had his wish. I spent an incredible amount of time with my father, and as an adult with children of my own I find it amazing how the majority was quality time. For someone that worked as much as he, there was always time for family. He loved to travel, and camp. His love for the water was unbelievable. He shared all of that with his family. He surrounded himself with his wife and his children. For someone who didn't experience life with a lot of siblings, he seemed to have it down to an art. Daddy made sure I had a solid spiritual foundation; God was always first in his house. He taught me how to use tools, and taught me his recipe for the best Chicken Noodle soup known to mankind. If I had to give a description, my father has lived a life as close to Christ as he could.

Love from my dad has always been unconditional. His best quality was the ability to allow you to make your mistake, listen to you, advise you accordingly and send you back to try again. Growing up in a diverse world that isn't so diverse was very interesting living with a man like daddy. There were times when prejudice was unbearable, but daddy always had just the right words for whatever the situation called for. When I was a little girl there was a park that was a few blocks from our house. The white adults at the park near our home never wanted us to play there, they would chase us out, and call us horrible names, but daddy told us we could play there. I remember him telling me "You are the best, you are a McCoy, and there is no one better than you." I later learned that meant, "If you don't love yourself, no one else will."

Daddy and I shared many conversations about what I wanted to do when I grow up, and not one day of my adult life has he ever told me that I didn't make it. Daddy was strict beyond belief, and by the book, but the love was always overflowing. Anytime an injury occurred and that was quite often he would ask me, "Why did you hurt me?" I was always confused because I was the one bleeding. Then he would send me to my mom for patchwork and be there after the clean up with cookies; somehow beyond the band aids I always felt better just knowing he was there for me and felt my pain. Waking up in the middle of the night with aches and pains always got warm milk or hot chocolate. It never mattered the time of night, daddy just got up and looked after me until I was ready to go back to sleep.

Sundays has always been an important day at my parent's house. It's the one day everyone in the family would come together. When I was young I didn't understand why my older brothers and sisters would invade my space by coming over and spending the entire day with us, but as an adult I too fell into sequence with our family tradition of Sunday dinner. I now understand that it is the one opportunity every week to fellowship with my entire family. I've learned to appreciate where I have come from, and our children understand what family is really all about. My mom cooked every Sunday for everyone, and the meals were as good as the company. We would invent games to play like; Who am I, or have scavenger hunts. Both Momma and my brother Wade would play some our favorite songs and we would sing off key with no worries.

We never had to ask anyone to join us; we seemed to be a party all by ourselves. A warm sunny Sunday never passed without a backyard barbeque. We would spend the entire evening just loving each other. I remember on the wall in the upstairs den was a light switch cover of a family sitting together at the dinner table and below it said, "A family that prays together stays together: Daddy has always been a strong enforcer when it came to that. Prayer is the foundation.

Daddy always had an explanation for anything that I was too young to understand. All questions had answers. I once ask, "How did you get that long scar on your back?" He looked at me with raised eyebrows, and told me it happened one day in the Amazon. A ferocious lion, tiger and bear attacked me." He told me how they tried to overtake him but he was successful in his fight. I can remember telling all of the other kids in my neighborhood, "My dad has fought bears and lions and have the scars to prove it." I was nineteen years old when I found out that he had surgery before I was born. He use to tell me he was made of steel, and although I now know what actually happened to him, a part of me still holds on to that wonderful story. Daddy is my hero, the one man that taught me respect is what you are, not what you demand.

My mother has also always been a very important part of my life, but daddy didn't leave her much room for nurturing when it came to me. Throughout my life daddy never went anywhere without momma, stuck like glue, two peas in a pod, inseparable. I used to wonder how momma must have felt. Daddy spending most of his time relating with his children, while momma was taking care of everything else. Momma was the behind the scenes kinda girl, while daddy was the enforcer/playmate. Daddy has always been a very loving father, yet he has also been the perfect example of a loving husband. He surrounded himself with his children, but momma always came first. He was never shy about declaring his love for momma to anyone. He only wanted to do what momma wanted to do. Whatever momma wanted momma got. I will always believe they were made for each other.

There were so many things that my mother didn't have to do because daddy was always so willing. Even on a bad day when they were upset with each other about something, daddy would go sit in the living room and momma would go to the kitchen. That's about the distance they would part. When I think about my childhood I remember, homemade ice-cream, drive-in movies, campfires, fishing, boat rides, amusement parks, vacation bible school, church, roller skating, Saturday trips to the eastern Market, hugs, kisses, laughter, picnics, holiday parties, Christmas music, the smell of tangerines, pecans, pancake breakfast, Abbott & Costello, bike riding, Niagara Falls, long drives in the car listening to Love Unlimited Orchestra, and building things in the backyard; all with daddy and momma. When my behavior called for discipline daddy was never a slacker. I got my just rewards when I was bad as well as when I was good.

> "Listen, my sons, to a father's instruction, pay attention and gain understanding. I give you sound learning, so do not forsake my teaching. When I was a boy in my father's house still tender, and an only child of my mother, he taught me and said, lay hold of my words with all your heart; keep my commands and you will live. Get wisdom, get understanding, do not forget my words or swerve from them. Do not forsake wisdom, and she will protect you' love her, and she will watch over you. Wisdom is supreme; therefore get wisdom. Though it cost all you have, get understanding. Esteem her, and she

will exalt you' embrace her, and she will honor you. She will set a garland of grace on your head and present you with a crown of splendor. Listen, my son, accept what I say, and the years of your life will be many." (Proverbs 4: 1-10)

CHAPTER **2**

Grace

I AM THE eighth born of ten children. The baby girl and I spent most of my time acting like it. I didn't concern myself much when it came to everyone else's feelings. I always felt people never meant what they said. Daddy always said a man is only as good as his word and everyone seemed to manipulate words. I developed the attitude that people would let you down no matter what. I made up my mind I would never put my faith in anything or anyone. I would keep my guard up with everyone except my family, so that I would not have to expose my true self. I took pride in being brutally honest, but developed a lack for tact. I knew God, but refused to be a part of his program. I was known for, and took pride in being a hell raiser. I spent my teenage years being defiant, and rebellious. Once I reached adulthood my relationship with God started to evolve.

At the age of eighteen I became pregnant. Not married yet and not knowing what life had in store for me I ventured out on my own with my soon to be husband. There were complications, surgery, and hospitalization. The doctors informed me that I was carrying twins and one was dead. They tried to encourage me not to go through with my pregnancy because the other child faced a chance of birth defects. They wanted to do test to determine what defects would be present, but I refused because I was going to love whatever God blessed me with. I prayed for a healthy child and went on with my life. After the birth of my daughter Dahlia, whom I called sunshine throughout my entire pregnancy, I discovered the lines of communication were open with God. Dahlia has been a constant source of happiness for me her entire life. With Dahlia even a stormy rainy day was filled with sunshine. Daddy and I had a very long talk after I came home from the hospital. Daddy explained to me his only prayer was to see his children grow up to be productive adults. For a long time I thought I missed my mark, but I now understand being a productive adult is who you are, not what you do. Two and a half years later my son was born. Raymond was the name chosen for him. Another very complicated pregnancy which also included the miscarry of his twin and three months of bed rest, Raymond was born with asthma. Serious enough to keep him hospitalized most of the time. I prayed he would someday grow out of it. Although I'm still waiting I thank God for keeping him here with me. Once Raymond turned five the doctors started him on steroids, which helped his asthma some, but caused other problems.

> "Praise the Lord, O my soul; all my inmost being, praise his holy name. Praise the Lord O my soul, and forget not all his benefits—who forgives all your sins and heals all your diseases, who redeems your life from the pit and crowns you with love and compassion, who satisfies your desires with good things so that your youth is renewed like the eagles." (Psalm 103: 1-5)

Through my entire experience with a sick child Raymond has also been a source of sunshine, a blessing; God's way of showing that only he can make the impossible possible. During my pregnancy we were at my parent's house for Sunday dinner there was company from out of town visiting and everything was quite festive. While fixing my dinner plate I started having cramps. It frightened me because I was only three months pregnant. I went to the bathroom where I noticed traces of blood. After thirty minutes passed the cramping was strong and hard, and the bleeding was heavy. My husband rushed me to the hospital where the doctors explained I was having a miscarriage. I began to cry because I fell in love with the fact of being pregnant. The doctors told me at this point the only thing to do were to have a D. & C. They paged my doctor and I waited patiently with a broken heart. Dr. Sai appeared and told me she was sorry. During my pelvic exam she called for a nurse to bring in a heart monitor. After placing the monitor on my abdomen we all heard a heartbeat. Dr. Sai then ordered an ultra sound, which showed a baby was still present. I cried knowing that God has a plan, and thanked God for being with me. I spent the next three months in the bed, but I knew with God's help happiness would be here soon. Daddy has always been very supportive when it came to Raymond's health. Always there with just the right words. Daddy told me to do what you need to do today, and say what you need to say today. I certainly hope my children are listening.

One month before Raymond's first birthday, I returned to the workforce. Eager and happy about having conversations with other adults. I managed to get the perfect job, with the most perfect boss in the world. Patrick is what everyone called him, and I too fell in love with his wisdom, kind nature and generosity. It is a family owned business, which means family operated. I didn't mind. The entire family was wonderful. I spent years working my way through the company and up the ladder. I eventually made my way to the highest level of management within the company. Patrick was very family oriented and I was allowed to raise my children within the walls of their corporate structure.

※※※

After twelve years of marriage my husband Ray and I divorced. It was an event that should have never happened, meaning we were so young we didn't know ourselves. We agreed to marry for all the wrong reasons. When we discussed marriage Ray was very honest in telling me that he felt I would make a great wife, just later in life, and I knew I wanted to have more children, but wanted my children to have the same father. So I gave Ray an ultimatum. Either we married now, or I continue my life with my child alone. God was never in the mist of our decisions nor did I consult God, which allowed the relationship to be very destructive. How could God keep my marriage together when we never made him a part of our relationship? We grew up, but not together, lacking the maturity to truly understand the magnitude of my marriage vows, love for my children was not enough. Despite my behavior, Ray did not want to divorce, but I knew if I stayed I would never grow to be the best I could be. Despite Ray's beliefs I also acknowledged I was not the one to bring out the best in him, I was determined to free myself from my self induced misery. This was a very difficult and painful time in my life. Prior to my separation I had never lived alone, and that seemed to really worry daddy. He asked me if I would come home to live with him and momma, but the thought of having an eleven o'clock curfew at the age of thirty was just a bit much. I declined and continued my journey on independence highway. Through the course of the years my parents were always there for me. My mom with the Kleenex, and daddy had the words of wisdom and kindness.

> "Do not judge, or you too will be judged, for in the same way you judge others, you will be judged, and with the measure you use, it will be measured to you. Why do you look at the speck of sawdust in your brother's eye and pay no attention to the plank in your own eye? How can you say to your brother, let me take the speck out of your eye, when all the time there is a plank in your own eye? You hypocrite, first take the plank out of your own eye, and then you will see clearly to remove the speck from your brother's eye." (Matthew 7:1-5)

Although everyone would gather on Sundays at my parents, all the children would also visit during the week when possible. During one of my visits I noticed something a little different about daddy's attitude. He seemed a little uneasy. He started talking about dreams he was having, vivid dreams that were very disturbing to him. I listened, tried to comfort him, but couldn't offer any solution. Having a moment alone with my mother I questioned her about daddy's dreams. She told me not to worry everything was fine. I didn't address the issue again.

As time passed I remember hearing daddy speak of his dreams more openly and quite frequently. It appeared the medicine that daddy was taking to control his hand tremors was causing his vivid nightmares; a simple side effect. I never thought to read the information pamphlet that came with his prescription. My sister Raina took my parents to the doctor and his medicine was changed. The dreams subsided, and things were back to normal.

Time passed and during visits daddy started to mention things he was seeing in the house. I didn't know what to do or say, but I thank God for my sisters and brothers. More doctors appointments, and more tests. We didn't have a clue what was in store for us.

During daddy's physical the doctor discovered daddy's PSA was well above normal. PSA stands for Prostate Specific Antigen. Through blood test your PSA is measured to check for enlarged prostate glands, or prostate cancer which is commonly found in elderly men. After the biopsy we were informed that daddy has prostate cancer. I was overwhelmed. Imagine that, I was overwhelmed. The word cancer has such a tone of death. I cried for days, feeling devastated. I told my best friend Randy about my dad's condition. He told me, "Now is the time to pray."

> Dear Lord,
> Daddy is very sick
> Please make him well
> I need him
> Heal his body, give him strength
> Amen

We had a family meeting, and as I said before God doesn't give you a task without the proper tools to complete the task decently and in order. Raina and Tamera were appointed to oversee daddy's care, and my brother Malcolm took over as the family glue, because daddy was dealing with a personal crisis. Little did I know prostate cancer was the smaller hurdle for me. I talked to Randy again and he told me now is a good time to pray, so we prayed together and waited.

Dear Lord,
We come before your throne of mercy
Humbly
Asking for you to bless this man
With recovery
Heal is body, and make shim strong again
Give us the strength and courage
To Endure
Thank you Lord for being such a merciful God.
In the name of Jesus
Amen.

Randy was always very supportive, and I found great comfort when we prayed together. God blessed daddy with successful surgery, and rewarding recovery. I had no idea I was being pruned for whatever else God needed me to do.

Daddy Recovered from the prostate cancer, and I am pleased to say today he is cancer free. In my mind that meant my hero is back on the block. A period of time passed and I was confronted with the choice of a lifetime. Randy, whom had become my best friend, asked me to marry him. I looked at this man before me, not on bended knee, but on bended knees. I shook my head yes as the tears rolled down my face. I thought to myself, God is in the mist of this, I can grow in God with this man, and Randy brings out the best in me. Daddy is better, Raymond's asthma is under control for now, and my best friend just proposed. At that moment I felt such peace in my heart.

After I mouthed the word yes, He explained to me that he needed my father's permission and blessing to close the deal.

The following Sunday Randy asked my father for my hand in marriage, and daddy explained to him, being a God fearing man was all he could ask of any man marrying one of his girls. He then asked Randy if he had any children. Randy replied, "Two boys." Daddy replied, "Well, boys are nice, but there is nothing in the world like having girls. Your girls will always come running to take care of you." Daddy shook Randy's hand gave me a hug and offered his blessing. Momma smiled with approval and we waited for everyone else to arrive so we could give them all the good news. After intense counsel, and prayer with our pastor; Raymond I. Austin; we decided to marry the first of spring. With only weeks to spare the planning began, and the time passed quickly. Before we knew it the day before the wedding was here. Everyone was present and on time. Daddy was very quiet during rehearsal, but I was so busy with everything else I never took the time to ask if everything was okay.

> "But do not forget this one thing, dear friends; with the Lord a day is like a thousand years, and a thousand years are like a day. The Lord is not slow in keeping his promise, as some understand slowness. He is patient with you, not wanting anyone to perish, but everyone to come to repentance." (2Peter 3:8-9)

On my wedding day Daddy walked me down the aisle and I felt such a sense of security. Daddy walked with certainty, and seemed quite relieved. That made me very happy. I was marring a man just like my dad. A man that Loves God, and cherish me. Daddy should be happy too. All of his girls were married to God fearing men much like himself. Our family continued to grow and Sunday dinner was just like thanksgiving.

One Sunday afternoon during our usual dinner discussion daddy walked into the dining room and called each of us out by name. He motioned us to come into his bedroom so he could talk to us alone. He seemed panicked, and that frightened me. I could feel a storm coming.

He started telling us about all the things going on in the house that he is seeing; people that he didn't know, things coming out of the light fixtures. "I won't let them move this!" The more he talked the less I understood. "They are trying to take things" he spoke with certainty. He seemed frightened, and vulnerable. He wanted us to believe him, anyone, and everyone. When he was finish talking, he turned and left the room. I suddenly felt a pain. It was coming from my chest. My heart was breaking. There was a moment of silence. No one spoke a word and one by one walked out of the room. For the first time in my life I felt helpless, and alone.

The rest of the family was sitting throughout the house; some in the den watching television, while others sat in the dining room in conversation. The grandchildren were playing cards, and enjoying each other. I questioned myself, why didn't momma come into the bedroom with daddy? Why hasn't she told somebody what was going on? I could see everything going on around me, but there seemed to be no sound. I wondered what is going on here, my brother Shamar put on his coat and left. At that moment I turned and looked at my brother Malcolm. He had tears in his eyes. At that very moment it was confirmed. It wasn't my imagination. Something was very wrong, and something had to be done. I walked into the living room, because I could no longer hold back the tears, which were forcing themselves from my eyes.

The entire tone of the day changed, conversations ceased. Some even left. Others found quiet places for solitude. Daddy went into the kitchen with momma and sat with a look of confusion and fright, not saying another word to anyone. Randy came into the living room and asked me, "What's wrong?" As I tried to explain the events of the previous fifteen minutes, Randy didn't seem to understand. I finally said, "There is something wrong with daddy!" Randy looked into my eyes and said, "I say it's time we pray."

That's when my silence began. I felt no one could ever understand what I am feeling.

Lord,
What's happening here?
I don't understand
Help me Lord
Make things the way they were, please God.

If ever there was the need for a rewind button I wished there were now.

"I sought the Lord, and he answered me; he delivered me from all my fears. Those who look to him are radiant; their faces are never covered with shame. This poor man called, and the Lord heard him; he saved him out of all his troubles. The angel of the Lord encamps around those who fear him, and he delivers them. Taste and see that the Lord is good; blessed is the man who takes refuge in him. Fear the Lord, you his saints, for those who fear him lack nothing." (Psalm 34: 4-9)

We agreed to have a family meeting, to decide what plan of action we needed to take. Malcolm changed the light fixtures, throughout the house, and Raina made doctor's appointments. Raina and Cadence took momma and daddy to the doctor. Raina informed me so I could also go, but I avoided attending. I selfishly felt the need to withdraw.

A week passed and during the next family meeting we were told that daddy needed more extensive test to find out the cause of what was happening. We scheduled for the next available appointment and waited. Once daddy was told he needed to return to the doctor for more extensive test, he totally refused to be seen by another doctor. We kept trying to convince daddy to go. It was time for God to step in.

Sleep seemed hard to come by anymore. My appetite was gone. Late one night Randy woke me because I seemed to be having a nightmare. First my vision was double, then my vision blurred, I panicked because I couldn't see. Randy rushed me to the hospital where I was immediately examined. I was transferred to the main hospital because of a possible stroke. After performing the necessary test the doctors couldn't find anything abnormal and sent me home.

Early the next morning my telephone rang. That was not unusual because we would sometimes call each other before leaving for work. However Tamera did not sound quite like herself today. Without much conversation she told me daddy may have Alzheimer's. My mind was racing; I could now feel the tears rolling down my face. What am I going to do? How am I going to deal with this? What about tomorrow? There is no cure for Alzheimer's disease. I'm going to lose my daddy. I sat on the floor of my bathroom crying without even realizing all my thoughts selfishly began with me. I felt I was at an all time low, and needed someone to understand.

Randy was home from work, and I proceeded to explain everything that I was told. He said to m, "I say it's time we pray." The tears overflowed and I began to sob without control, because I needed him to hurt with me. Grasping at anything I screamed and cried because the pain was overwhelming and he wasn't crying with me. Then he explained.

God does everything for a reason; and you have to hold on to God's unchanging hand, he never leaves you alone. Now is the time to remain steadfast. The doctors don't know, but God does. I cried, Randy held me tight, and we prayed.

Dear Lord
Help us
Change our circumstance
Make daddy well

Give us strength and courage
Thank you Lord
For being God.

Going to work, family meetings, and raising children, all while taking care of my husband and home starting taking a toll on me. My job was my newly found outlet for my stress. I was able to talk to Patrick about everything going on, and he always had words of wisdom and comfort for me. His son Cain however lacked the same understanding. I needed to help my family through this. Cain's focus was strictly on business. I felt torn between obligations.

"For I know how many are your offenses and how great your sins. You oppress the righteous and take bribes and you deprive the poor of justice in the courts. Therefore the prudent man keeps quiet in such times, for the times are evil. Seek good, not evil, that you may live. Then the Lord God almighty will be with you, just as you say he is." (Amos 5: 12-14)

Once again before work, my phone rang. This time it was my mother. "Your daddy wants you to get over here now!" It was a cold morning, snow, sleet, and the roads were covered with ice. Tamera agreed to pick up Cadence, and I headed to Riana's house to get her. We arrived at my parent's house and my dad seemed worried. He explained his experiences of the previous night and wanted some relief. Everyone took the day off from work and stayed there with momma and daddy the entire day. After our arrival daddy seemed to relax, he even laid down in bed for a nap and I could tell he was glad his girls was there. Once again Raina and Tamera explained to daddy the importance of the test that the doctor recommended. His reservations about taking any test subside long enough for him to agree to go.

The morning of the test arrived quickly. I requested the day off from work. After fourteen years of dedication to my job Patrick understood and encouraged me to be there for my dad. I really needed to show daddy I was there for him. Through all of my feelings of being alone I realized for the first time momma is the one alone. She was the one that was dealing with this crisis. Momma was on the front line solid as a rock; standing right by daddy side. I told Randy that was what I needed right now. So Randy also took the day off from work to attend. Randy stood by my side solid as a rock, and I found great comfort in his kind gesture.

That was a very stressful day I thought. Those of us that could attend were there. The test took all day, and daddy was not happy. If I felt pressure, I could only imagine how daddy must have felt. He didn't even want to go. After the test was complete the doctor called the family in for a conference. Malcolm stayed in the lobby with daddy and Randy, while momma, Raina, Cadence, and I went to discuss the results. "His comprehension isn't very good, and he is confused about many things. We need to do more test in order to pin point which direction to go in." By the time the conference was over daddy was very agitated with everything and everyone. He took the papers, put on his coat and vowed never to return. We went to my parent's house for dinner and drove home in silence. Once again Randy and I prayed.

We all started spending more time at my parent's house than our own homes, but everything that's necessary isn't always pleasant. Time passed, I'm not sure how much, but every time there was a problem with daddy everyone just seemed to adjust. We spent more time with momma and daddy reading the bible, and praying together as a family. Then I received a phone call at work. "Daddy has Dementia" Tamera was crying, and I too lost my composure. We decided on a day, time and once again met to find answers and solutions.

CHAPTER **3**

What Is Dementia?

WHAT IS DEMENTIA? Dementia is the loss of mental functions—such as thinking, memory, and reasoning. Dementia develops when the parts of the brain that are involved with learning, memory, decision-making, and language are affected by one or more of a variety of infections or diseases. The most common cause of dementia is Alzheimer's disease.

What causes Dementia? Degenerative diseases of the nervous system, such as Alzheimer's, Lewy Body, Parkinson's, and Huntington's. Diseases that affect blood vessels, such as stroke, or multi-infarct dementia, which is caused by multiple strokes in the brain.

We discussed daddy's medical history and decided on a plan of action. We researched the present medication and decided on the best medicine with the least side effects. Although everyone visited regularly, we needed to create a visitation schedule that would not put everyone's lives in disarray. We decided on days to visit, and created a monthly calendar.

The first couple of weeks went well. Everyone was available and willing. By the third week the only constant visitors were Malcolm, Raina, Cadence, and I. The more everyone was there, the better daddy seemed to be. I think he needed the same amount of unconditional love, which he spent his entire life giving to his children from his children. As the weeks passed I grew very tired and my body felt weak. I could feel my patience growing short for everyone except daddy. Raymond's asthma was once again tormenting him. Time for more hospitalization, more medicine and more treatments. I noticed numbness in my right arm which didn't seem to affect anything I was doing, it was just a portion, not my entire arm. However it annoyed me enough to see my doctor. During my visit my doctor did not see any physical reason why this was happening, but ordered a test to check my nerves. The test went fine, and everything was normal. The doctor asked me if I was under any amount of stress. I laughed and said, "No more stress than any other person living on this planet."

After Raymond recovered, he decided that he wanted to live with his father. His father felt I put him second to Randy. I wasn't treating him the way they felt I should. I thought I was being a good mother, but I refused to neither give in to Raymond's demands nor allow his father to make decisions for my household. His father being a single dad had more personal time to devote to Raymond, my only issue with part time parenting is four days a month anyone can devote their time to all fun and games, but full time parenting consists of much more. I was enforcing spiritual growth and the need for education. I fought tooth and nail to keep Raymond, but the courts felt Raymond was of legal age to decide which parent he wanted to live with. I felt I was being punished for marrying Randy, and because of this choice, my life with my son would never again be the same. It broke my heart when he left. Randy and I left to take his son Marcus home after a weekend visit. While we were gone Raymond called his dad to pick him up. He packed his things and left like a thief in the night. I was very bitter and angry about it. That made it easier to close everyone in my life out emotionally. I spent time with everyone, but I refused to deal with any emotions. Randy and daddy, and Dahlia were the only persons I allowed in my heart.

"And then he said; "I tell you the truth, unless you change and become like little children, you will never enter the kingdom of heaven. Therefore, whoever humbles himself like this child is the greatest in the kingdom of heaven. And whoever welcomes a little child like this in my name welcomes me. But if anyone causes one of these little ones who believe in me to sin, it would be better for him to have a large millstone hung around his neck and to be drowned in the depths of the sea." (Matthew 18: 3-6)

꩜꩜꩜

  I continued talking to daddy about things that I felt but didn't understand. He still gave me kind words, something soft and loving. I have always loved the way daddy talked to me. With love and total approval. One evening we were in the middle of a conversation and from nowhere daddy started telling Randy how very special I have always been. "Eliana has always worked hard and done well." Daddy smiled, "she has overcome great odds and made the best of everything in her life." At that that moment I wished I could have bottled the words of approval, appreciation, love and compassion from daddy.

  My moments of solitude seemed filled with emotional pain. Never have I ever felt this helpless. My son left me. Rejected by the child whom I bared, feeling abandoned by someone I would have never abandoned. All while my dad is sick, with dementia. Although it was never discussed at our family meetings through all my research I knew one day this path would lead daddy to Alzheimer's.

  Time passed, and each week I found myself spending less time at my parent's house. I didn't feel necessary, I felt like a visitor. When the family was around, an outsider, I felt like I was out of the circle. I quietly blamed everyone for my personal pain. That wasn't even the worst part. I tried to put all of my feelings in a bundle and give them to Randy to deal with. I was no longer going to emotionally deal with anything. I developed a distant attitude toward everyone in my life. I no longer had the drive to even get my work done, which was a high production management position. I even started pushing Randy away.

Without realizing where my mind was most of the time we continued to pray.

> Dear Lord
> I know you can hear me
> What am I doing wrong?
> Please help me
> Speak to my heart, Tell me
> What do you want me to do?

What was I praying for? I was asking God to perform a miracle on my life by changing the mess I created within myself. Bless daddy with good health, long life, comfort and happiness. I became overwhelmed with daddy and his happiness. I would get so mad at Randy when he seemed to lack understanding. If I couldn't make it to my parents house on Sundays; I would tell Randy things like, "Daddy's not going to be here forever. When my parents are gone we can do whatever you like." I was blaming my attitude and actions on him, but he was the only supportive person left in my life. Who else was there for me to turn away?

> "Ask and it will be given to you; seek and you will find, knock and the door will be opened to you. For everyone who asks receive; he who seek find; and to him who knocks, the door will be opened. (Matthew 7: 7-8)

The end of the year came with much surprise. Randy's grandson came to live with us. What an adjustment. Samuel brought a sense of normalcy back into my life. I called him Gummi Bear. For Samuel brought to me all the joy a new life could. All of my heart that I needed to give I could give to Samuel. He wouldn't reject me, because he needed me also. Nor was he suffering from some illness that would require me to let him go. Randy and Dahlia were always very helpful with Samuel's care, and I no longer had to deal with the reality of my life's circumstances.

Dear Lord
Thank you for sending Samuel
I needed to feel loved
Unconditionally
You have sent me a part of yourself
Thank you
I love you Lord, Amen.

Once again I noticed my body was weak, and I always seemed tired, but having Samuel in our home brought so much joy I overlooked everything I was feeling, and put all of my spare time into him. Randy and I took Samuel everywhere we went. Dahlia also gave all of her spare time and attention to Samuel. Before my very eyes God was creating a family bond of courage, strength, and endurance. At night when Samuel would wake, Randy would get out of bed and care for him. Change his diapers, feed him and rock him back to sleep. I saw my father's love for me when I watched randy with Samuel. I thank God every day for sending Samuel to us. All the things Randy and I didn't experience by having children together had been delivered.

Raymond would come to visit two weekends out of every month. Although we would talk, I felt a sense of resentment towards him. I would care for him while he was visiting, but kept him at a distance from my heart. Our conversations were brief and direct, and I refused to relate to anything he was going through. It appeared his father Ray had to trade his part-time, let's have fun parenting in for being a full time parent, and Raymond seemed remorseful. I totally disassociated myself from my own son. Late one night Raymond called for help, because he was having an asthma attack. He explained his father would not take him to the hospital, because he did not feel it was bad enough. I was so bitter that for a moment I felt that was their problem. I was not getting out of my bed to drive across town to pick up my son that should be living with me in the first place, and drive him to the hospital. Randy told me there was no reason for Raymond to pay for his mistakes with his life. We drove over, picked Raymond up and took him to Children's Hospital. Little did I know it was the first of many late night pickups to drive Raymond to the hospital for his asthma, while his dad lay in the bed sleeping. Once again Raymond was hospitalized, and although I visited him daily I didn't stay at the hospital with him like I used to. When Raymond was discharged I left the decisions of his care to him and his dad. I felt it was something for them to learn to deal with. Raymond would call to talk to me, but my bitterness towards him and his father would not allow me to have more than a brief conversation with him. Unfortunately I was penalizing Raymond for his father's actions. I was back to visiting my parents only on Sundays and my heart to heart conversations with daddy seemed to just stop. I missed talking to daddy, but he didn't seem to notice. I was so busy feeling sorry for my circumstances. I didn't even take the time to make the time to spend in conversation with anybody.

Daddy appeared to be doing better; I was glad the medicine was working. There were activities that we found on the internet that would help with his condition. Tamera would go over and walk with daddy when the weather would permit. Cadence played checkers with daddy, and spent time singing the songs that daddy loved while momma played the piano, and Malcolm was always there to repair and replace anything. When there was nothing to be done, Malcolm was there just because. Daddy could always depend on Raina to stop by for good conversation and a good meal. I continued to spend most of my time at home caring for my little Gummi Bear. I continued to pray, but I was asking God for the same things as before.

Dear Lord,
Thank you for Randy
Thank you for Samuel
Thank you for Dahlia
Please make daddy well
Give me the strength to endure
May your will be done, Amen.

After ten months Samuel went home to live with his mom and dad. I cried for days, I was so attached to him. He loved me like daddy and Randy; no restrictions. I didn't realize that restrictions were what I put on everyone. No one was allowed to get too close. Even when I opened my heart, I put restrictions on the love which I was to receive from everyone.

Although Samuel went home it didn't seem to change anything between us; during his ten month visit we created a special bond which can never be broken. We saw Samuel as often as we wanted and he continued to spend time with us. With Samuel living at home with his parents once again I was alone and forced to deal with the circumstances of my life.

The fall season was drawing near. The weather was changing. Randy's sister Lachelle was home visiting from Texas. She wanted to help take care of Randy's brother George whom was quite ill after suffering from a stroke. During Lachelle's visit she died suddenly. The doctors told us it was a massive heart attack. A tragedy I didn't think I was prepared to deal with. Randy seemed lost, hurt, and confused. I did everything I could to make things easy for him. Randy always provided me with the support I needed. He was always there for me with prayer, love, or just silence. It was now my turn to hold things together.

With the help and support of our church family, and our dear friend and Pastor, we were able to get through Lachelle's home going ceremony. Pastor Austin stepped in and helped, offering prayer and encouragement to Randy and myself. During the family hour my lifelong friend Becky, whom has known my family since my children were babies sat beside my parents. She spoke to my mom and dad. Daddy spoke politely; buy did not know who she was. After about thirty minutes daddy looked at Becky spoke to her and said he was happy to see her. Becky looked confused, but didn't question anything.

When I spoke to Becky later she asked how my dad was doing. I neglected to inform her about daddy condition, and told her he just didn't know who she was. I thanked God for blessing me with such a supportive family Becky included, and tried to help Randy deal with his grief.

Four months later Randy's brother George died in his sleep from cerebral hemorrhage. This was very devastating for Randy. We hadn't recovered from the death of his sister. I tried to handle everything; I didn't want Randy to buckle under the stress of loss. I tried to embrace and protect Randy from the pain of his loss. I saw in Randy all the love that my father has for my mother his dependence on her and her significant role in his life. Once again Pastor Austin and our church family were there to our rescue. I felt physically exhausted, my body was weak, there was numbness in my upper right leg; Patrick's son Cain was demanding I work overtime, Raymond was sick, and daddy was losing his memory. After the ceremony, I was sitting in a chair. Pastor Austin was offering final remarks and prayer. I felt a pain, a rush, dizziness. It felt like my heart was exploding. I felt I could no longer deal with anything going on in my life. I cried uncontrollably in the arms of Randy Jr., unable to stop.

I'm sure everyone thought I was crying because George was dead. I was hurt and very sad over the loss of George. We didn't always see eye to eye, but I loved him. We shared some very special moments together before he died. However my tears were the result of the pain I felt in my heart, my life seemed to be in constant turmoil. I closed my eyes and silently talked to God. "I surrender Lord; please help me to deal with everything you have given me. Bless me with wisdom and understanding." There was a moment of solitude, then a revelation. God only gives us as much as we can bear words of comfort to me.

> "Therefore we do not lose heart. Though outwardly we are wasting away, yet inwardly we are being renewed day by day. For our light and momentary troubles are achieving for us an eternal glory that far outweighs them all. So we fix our eyes not on what is seen, but on what is unseen. For what is seen is temporary, but what is unseen is eternal." (2Corinthians 4: 16-18)

That Sunday I visited my parents. I needed to talk to daddy. I tried to explain to him what I was feeling, and for the first time he didn't listen to me. He only wanted to know how Randy was doing. He told me it is my responsibility to take care of him. I tried to tell him how I felt, and that's when daddy said, "You don't understand sometimes it's not about how you feel, it's about how Randy feels, you still have your entire family. When my brother died I had so many unresolved issues. I should have never let any time pass between us." From that moment on I tried to be more understanding of everyone else feelings including daddy's.

⁂

Once again I sat in my doctor's office complaining of numbness in my right leg. My Doctor explained because I was under a lot of stress I needed to take some time out for myself. She ordered more tests and put me on medication for my blood pressure, which was exceedingly high.

One month later we were blessed with the home of our dreams. Randy and I had been attending weekly bible study and we continued to pray. I learned I needed to be more in tune with God's will instead of my own. And the only way to learn Gods will is by learning God's word. After we received the keys to our new home Tamera brought my parents by to see what the Lord has blessed us with.

Daddy walked through the entire house with a smile on his face. He told me he was very proud of us, and the sacrifice it must have taken to make such an achievement. Randy told daddy we could have never accomplished this without God. Once again I was happy with daddy's approval.

> "Bring the whole tithe into the storehouse, that there may be food in my house. Test me in this, says the Lord Almighty, and see if I will not throw open the floodgates of heaven and pour out so much blessing that you will not have room enough for it." (Malachi 3:10)

Daddy's moods continued to change; he was more silent and less involved on Sundays. Randy and I continued to pray, and we would visit their church regularly. Every year their church would hold an annual family and friend's day. This year our family decided to attend. My parents had about twenty guests in attendance. Daddy seemed so proud. He is always happiest when he has his family together. It always pleased me to see daddy happy.

Dear Lord,
Thank you for Randy
Thank you for Dahlia
Thank you for our home
Thank you for being God
Make Daddy well
May your will be done, Amen.

During a Barbeque at our house, we decided to have an appreciation dinner for my brother Malcolm. He always seemed to go above and beyond when it came to his family. He never asked for anything in return. Malcolm much like daddy took an active role in my childhood. I remember days of fishing. Malcolm taught me the patience of fishing. Once a week he took Wade, Shamar and me to the movies. I was with Malcolm when I discovered I didn't like scary movies. Malcolm also had a large part of my heart. We picked a date, place and time, and the planning began. My parents agreed to attend, but didn't like to be out after dark.

Easter was the only holiday before Malcolm's appreciation dinner. We decided on our menu, and looked forward to another family gathering. However Easter dinner was not as pleasant as expected. Everyone was there, but daddy didn't seem like himself. I noticed he appeared angry, and not very happy to see anyone. I questioned what was wrong, but neither daddy nor momma would talk. After supper daddy said he was tired and was going to bed. This was quite unusual and I didn't understand. We all left early and my feelings were hurt.

Randy and I prayed, but this time I prayed that God would show me what was wrong and what I needed to do to make it right.

> Dear Lord,
> Thank you for today
> Help momma and daddy deal with this
> Draw me nearer to you Lord
> Change me Lord
> I love you, Amen.

Once again I started visiting my parents more during the week. Daddy's attitude was fine during the week, but he seemed agitated when I would visit on Sundays.

The night of the appreciation dinner was wonderful. Everyone was there. There were speeches, and song. Malcolm cried; he was really surprised. My parents came and found a quiet place to sit. Everyone that attended was lifelong friends of the family or relatives. Daddy was silent, and withdrawn.

I noticed and wanted to talk with him, but was too busy trying to take care of everything else. After our family prayer, and before dinner was served daddy and momma decided to go home. I was sad that they wouldn't stay, but it was dusk, and I knew they wanted to go.

Once the weather changed it was time for flowers and housework. I was so excited to plant my first flower garden at our new home. The yard needed a lot of work, and I was willing to exert as much time and effort as necessary. It took up most of my free time, and kept me from dealing with daddy's condition, and Raymond's behavior.

❧❧❧

Every first Sunday Randy and I spent the day at church, Wednesdays we attended bible study, and Saturday we worked in the yard. The other days were for laundry, cleaning and working around the house. We managed to go to my parent's house on our free Sundays. Once a month we held a family night out to dinner, so momma wouldn't have to cook. I was very grateful they always planned them around first Sunday's, because Randy and I would not be able to attend. It was always wonderful to go out with my entire family, but daddy was always silent.

Raina decided this summer's family event would be a chili cook-off. We would all enter our own secret recipes, and judges would decide whose chili was the best. We picked a chili cook-off date, and bragged about whose chili was going to win.

About a week later I received a call at work. "Don't panic, don't get upset, momma fell, Tamera is there, and taking them to the hospital." I was calm, but very concerned. I asked what happen. Raina explained momma slipped on water in the basement while doing the laundry. I left work with Cain objecting, heading for the hospital. When I arrived daddy was sitting in the lobby with Malcolm and Tamera. He seemed very concerned and quiet. Raina arrived shortly after, and daddy was relieved to see her. The doctors needed x-rays, and they gave momma medicine for pain which made her very drowsy. Tamera and Raina continued to spend time with momma in her room. I finally gained the courage to go back to see her. The doctor was there, and explained her condition. Nothing was broken, only her tailbone was bruised. They gave her more medicine and I went to the Lobby to report the good news. I explained to daddy what was going on, but he kept repeating what I was saying as though he didn't understand. I asked daddy if he wanted to see her. He said he didn't want to go back just yet. Cadence and Shamar arrived shortly after, and I took Cadence back and left her there. When she came back to the lobby she was obviously upset. Raina explained to her that daddy did not need to see any of us upset, because that would upset him.

Raina decided to go back into her room. She returned quite quickly stating the medicine has made momma sick. She didn't want to be alone but Riana's stomach couldn't take it. Cadence tried to stay but she too couldn't with stand momma being ill. They looked at me and told me it was my turn.

I walked into her room, and momma was sleeping. I looked at

her and could never remember a time when I had to be there for her. I closed my eyes and prayed. I asked God to have his way with us. At that moment momma started to moan and once again had to vomit. I felt nauseous and light, but knew I had to be strong for my mother. I helped her as much as I could; the thoughts in my mind were strange. I am only doing for my mother all the things she has ever done for me. I tried to control my stomach and every now and then walk away from her room to get fresh air. Upon my return momma was sleeping, I looked at her and realized how very fragile she really is. Strong, stern, loving, always taking care of daddy. Always right by his side. I thought to myself, I want to be just like her when I grow up. Finally the doctor came in and told me she was able to go home. We only had to wait for her prescriptions, and discharge papers.

I went to the lobby and explained momma was ready to go, but because she was still throwing up no one wanted to go back and help dress her. Malcolm agreed to help get her into the wheel chair and to the car, but could not assist in helping with anything else. It had to be one of the girls. I found myself elected.

Daddy and I went into momma's room where she was sleeping at that time. She still had her I-V, and the nurse hadn't been in her room yet. Daddy looked at her and called her name. "Wake up Tammy" he said as he gently rubbed her face. I touched his arm, "Daddy it's the medicine, she can't wake up just yet." Daddy looked at me and then once again looked at momma, "Wake up! You have to get up now!" Listening to daddy pleading, and watching him with his wife, my heart hurt. I needed to control my tears. "God help me to be strong" I whispered, "Daddy relies on her, he needs her." All the things I knew as a child I was witnessing right now. Daddy looked at me and asked, "Why won't she wake up?" Again I explained, "It's the medicine, she can't wake up just yet." A few moments later he tried to wake her again. Then I understood; daddy doesn't understand what's going on.

Once the nurse arrived she removed the I-V and the discharge papers were signed. By this time daddy was very agitated and wanted to go home. He got momma to wake, and he and I dressed her.

He fussed at me the entire time and I was more frustrated than ever. Malcolm put momma into Riana's car and we followed them home. Malcolm then went to pick up dinner while we tried to get momma dressed for bed. Daddy was busy looking for his keys, which were in his hand. We tried to explain that to him, but he was tired, frustrated, and hungry. Daddy also had not taken any of his medication since morning. Once we were able to get momma to bed it was time for daddy's medicine. Cooperation was not a factor, and the evening was getting worse by the minute. We didn't know which pill he was suppose to take at what time. He had two sets of eye drops, and he refused to cooperate. Daddy wanted momma to take care of everything as she usually did, and right now it just wasn't possible. We were able to wake momma long enough to find out just what daddy was suppose to take. Once daddy saw her awake, with a little begging and pleading daddy decided to take his medicine. At that moment I learned it was our responsibility to know what medication to give daddy, what time, and how much. We needed to figure out a schedule, because momma would not be able to get around to cook, clean, and take care of daddy. The doctors said she would need at least two weeks of bed rest to heal. Momma explained that they have a light breakfast at five-thirty in the morning, a full breakfast at ten thirty, lunch around two o'clock, and dinner at six. With Dahlia away at college, and Raymond living with his father I am the only girl without children to take care of in the morning so I decided to take the first shift. By this time it was eleven o'clock and I didn't have much time left for rest. I rushed home crying all the way thanking God for momma. No one could ever care for daddy like her.

> Dear Lord,
> Thank you for being the type of God that
> Loves us in spite of ourselves
> Bless the sick
> And allow your light to shine through me
> Give me the strength, and courage to endure

Bless my husband, my family, and my home
Have your way with me
Guide and direct me
May your will be done on earth, as it is in heaven
Amen.

The next morning at four-thirty I rose from my sleep. Showered, dressed, and drove to my parent's house. I arrived at five fifteen, and daddy was at the door waiting for me. Daddy let the dog outside, and I put on water for breakfast. After making coffee I made cream of wheat. Daddy stood over my shoulder the entire time. While I was pouring the cream of wheat into the bowls, daddy looked at me and said, "That looks a little lumpy!" I thought to myself at five –thirty in the morning a few lumps should be okay. I smiled at daddy and said, "I don't see any lumps" as I smashed the lumps with my spoon. I poured the milk and served him his breakfast. Momma ate her breakfast with no complaints, took her medicine and dosed back off to sleep. After breakfast it was time for daddy to take his medicine. Daddy allowed me to put the eye drops in, but refused to take his pills. When I asked he said no. I just don't know how to be forceful with the man that laid all the laws in my childhood, and I have never experienced his stubbornness one on one before. I tried to talk daddy into taking it, but nothing would work. Malcolm arrived shortly after, made a grocery list and headed to the supermarket, Tamera brought breakfast at ten-thirty, Malcolm cleaned the kitchen as I laid down to take a nap. We rotated our schedules, and spent the next week cooking, cleaning, and pleading with daddy to take his medicine. Trying to care for daddy was very hard, because all he wanted was momma. After awhile momma was able to get around and daddy was once again his usual cooperative self. I learned you should always have a list of medications your love ones are taking without having to rely on someone else's knowledge. I f that someone else can't help you; you won't find yourself completely lost looking for answers. I was glad once momma was doing better; it allowed me to catch up on some much needed rest. I was feeling quite run down and very tired, but I still had so many things to do.

Once momma was feeling better it was time to have our chili cook-off. Everyone was participating. Because the cook-off had been previously cancelled it was held on a Sunday which Randy and I could not participate. I was a little disappointed, but understood. We promised to be there as early as we could, and things seem to be back to normal. It was a beautiful sunny Sunday afternoon, and I was so excited. By the time we arrived at my parent's house the judging was over, daddy was upset and everyone was leaving. I went into the living room and asked Raina what was going on. She told me someone spilled chili on the tablecloth and it really seemed to upset daddy really bad. He kept asking how we are going to get the chili out of the tablecloth. I returned to the kitchen and tried to talk to daddy, but he would not talk to me. The more I tried to talk to him the angrier he became. I tried to talk to momma, but she only said, "You know how you father is." I didn't understand, and I couldn't get any answers, so I gathered my things and went home. I was angry because I didn't know what was going on and I wasn't there to see for myself.

Daddy seemed to be agitated for a few days afterward, but as the weeks progressed he seemed to be feeling better. I was tired all of the time, but felt a need to maintain. Randy and I continued to pray, and I waited for my answers.

My visits to the doctor seemed regular, however outside of my blood pressure she could find nothing wrong. I was starting to question my sanity. I know what I was feeling, and my body was trying to tell me something, but I wasn't sure what. Every time I was tested for anything, everything was normal.

CHAPTER 4

What's Wrong with Me?

THE SUMMER WAS filled with good days and bad days with daddy. He would call in a panic, and we would come running. As the seasons changed so did daddy's condition. He starting forgetting things and people, wanting to go places he had been in days past. Daddy talked a lot about going home, I assumed he meant his birth home in Georgia, I would soon find out where this home was.

Daddy always seemed happier once we arrived and we were more than happy to be there. I continued to suppress my feelings and worries about my health. I avoided sharing them with everyone except Randy at all costs. It seemed all the running back and forth started to take its toll, I have never felt so tired and drained of energy in my life, and Randy suggested I make another visit to our family doctor. During my visit Dr. Vang once again questioned if I was under any stress. I had to laugh as I explained to her my father's condition and my work environment. She suggested more tests and I went home to my family.

Thanksgiving was here before I knew it. I cooked dinner as usual, but we always ate dinner at my parent's house. We were sitting at the table enjoying a marvelous meal when I had an excruciating pain in my forehead. I started to cry and then I became sick to my stomach. Randy rushed me to the hospital. The doctors performed a spinal tap, which was normal; they prescribed medication for the pain, and sent me home to rest. Because of the demands for my time at work, I didn't know what to do about my job. Cain called me at home and demanded I return to work immediately. I attempted to go, but the pain and exhaustion would not allow my body to get around. Once I explained to Randy what was going on he called Cain and explained that my health was more important to him than any job I could ever hold. He told him I was staying home until I was better, and if they needed to replace me now is the time. It was agreed that I would have a couple of days off to recover. After I felt better I returned to work. Cain was very unforgiving for my time off, but knew it was best for me to return. The work hours were long, and I was doing all that I could to juggle work, home, Randy, daddy, and my tired weak body.

The season changed and I finally started getting used to things at hand. Randy and I continued to pray, but as I grew in faith and read God's word my spirit started to evolve. I was no longer asking God to change daddy's situation, but to change me to better deal with daddy the way he is. Open my mind, touch my heart, and walk my path with me.

> Dear Lord,
> I love you, and adore you
> Change me to be what you want me to be
> Forgive me for all my sins,
> Instead of moving my mountain
> Help me to climb my mountain
> Let everyone who look at me see you
> Bless my husband, my family, and my home
> Have your way with me
> Guide and direct me, bless all who teaches your word
> In Jesus name, Amen.

"Blessed are the poor in spirit, for theirs is the kingdom of heaven. Blessed are those who mourn, for they will be comforted. Blessed are the meek, for they will inherit the earth.

Blessed are those who hunger and thirst for righteousness, for they will be filled. Blessed are the merciful, for they will be shown mercy. Blessed are the pure in heart, for they will see God. Blessed are the peacemakers, for they will be called sons of God. Blessed are those who are persecuted because of righteousness, for theirs is the kingdom of heaven." (Matthew 5: 3-10)

◆◆◆◆

I continued to visit my parents with my newfound perspective in life, and then it happened.

I was sitting in the kitchen with daddy looking out the window and he said to me, "I know that there is something wrong with me, and I don't like it. I can't do anything about it, and I'm tired." I could feel tightness in my chest as daddy continued. "I want to go home." I remembered lately when daddy wanted to go home he didn't recognize where he was, so we would put him in the car and drive him around until he recognized where he was and would direct us to the house. I thought to myself its dark outside and I don't want to take him out alone, so I told him, you are at home daddy." He said "I know that I am where I live, but I want to go home to be with my father." Daddy continued to tell me about the conversation he had earlier today with his brother John, and why he wanted to go home, I truly felt my heartbreak. Uncle John died twelve years ago and daddy looked sad and very tired. "Everything is going to be okay daddy." I said with the best smile I could muster. At that moment momma came into the kitchen and took daddy by the hand telling him it was time for bed. I watched my hero being led into his room and I could not hold my pain inside. I sat in a chair sobbing trying to stop what I was feeling and had no control. Dahlia drove me home that night.

When I arrived at home I went to my bedroom to lie down. I felt sick to my stomach, and could barely breathe. I started to vomit, and my chest hurt. I called to Dahlia, "Take me to the hospital now!"

Randy was working the afternoon shift and Dahlia could not

reach him. The doctors took me in and starting running test. They explained that I might have had a mild heart attack. For once in Dahlia's life she remained composed and started making phone calls. They explained I would have to stay and they were transferring me to the cardiac wing.

The next morning when I woke Randy was there. We had previously had an argument prior to him going to work the night before. He told me when they gave him my room number he was given the wrong section. The room he went into had a patient on a respirator. He said there were tubes and lines everywhere. He told me at that point he became very emotional, and realized nothing was more important to him than us.

We met with the cardiologist and they explained I needed a stress test, and a cardiac catherization to see the function of my heart. I was afraid, but Randy was there by my side the entire time. He informed Pastor Austin, and our church family of my condition. After the entire test was done the doctors told us that my ejection fraction is forty percent. Ejection fraction is the volume of blood the heart is pumping out with each heartbeat. A normal person's ejection fraction is sixty percent. I needed to be seen regularly by a cardiologist and was put on medication for my weak heart. Randy told me once again now is the time to pray.

> Is this it Lord,
> Is this what was wrong with me
> Life is so precious
> Please bless me with just one more day, if it is your will Lord
> Keep my family safe
> Bless my Pastor, his family, and our church
> Guide and Direct our path
> In Jesus name, Amen.

After spending time with my cardiologist I was diagnosed with Dilated Cardio Myopthy. This is the formal term for enlarged heart. It was caused by years of untreated hypertension. In other words what we do or don't do for our bodies, our bodies will do or will not do for us later in life.

My recovery was quick, and I was back to work dealing with matters at hand. I thank God for Patrick; he stepped in when I needed someone indirectly involved to talk to.

Daddy seemed very sad and talked about going home very often. His confusion was apparent, and his episodes of wanting to leave the house to go home were more frequent. We would take daddy for rides in the car, driving around until he would recognize the neighborhood. He would then direct us to the house and be content for a little while. His talk of going home prompted the family to plan a trip to Atlanta, Georgia, to the house daddy grew up in. The family would take a trip to Georgia yearly, and we knew Grandma would be very pleased to see us. We picked a date and made our travel arrangements

One Night I received a call from Raina. "Momma is crying she can't get daddy to calm down!" I rushed to the house and by the time I arrived everyone was there. Daddy was sitting at the kitchen table calm and quiet. Momma said, "He won't take any of his medicine." As daddy started speaking it was quite apparent he did not know who momma was. He kept referring to momma as he. Daddy thought that she was a man. I talked to daddy for a while, he was pleasant, knew I was one of his children, but he didn't know who I was. He was so cordial I couldn't be sure. I asked daddy to please take his pills and he replied, "I will not take any pills he (referring to momma) is trying to give me. He is consistently bothering me and I just want to be left alone." Daddy was so demanding I wasn't sure how to respond, or what to do, so I gave the pills to Tamera and told her to give it a try.

When Tamera approached daddy he immediately had a calming look on his face. He kept calling her Tammy, which is my mother's name. He thought that Tamera was my mother. This upset her because she did not know how to handle this. She told him to take the medicine because it would make him feel better. He took the pills from her and took them. Then he proceeded to fuss about the man (my mother) which was in his house. We tried to show him photographs from days gone by, and he recognized everyone in the photos except momma. I went into the dining room to take a breather. Malcolm was sitting in a chair crying. I felt his pain and wanted to hold him, but my body wouldn't move. I have always taken much pride in Malcolm's strength, and I wanted to be strong like him. In control of everything. I now see no one is in control except God.

The night was long, and I was extremely tired when I returned home. Randy was sleeping. I called Becky and finally told her what was going on with Daddy. She cried with me for an entire hour. I was able to finally address the fact that I was hurt, and angry. I thought I wanted what I considered to be my normal life back. Once I thought about it, my life before had peace, but no Christ. I then decided I wanted to keep the life I have with Christ, because he could give me blessed quietness. When I was finished I began to pray.

> Dear Lord,
> Thank you for another day
> My body is weak, my heart hurts
> I know you have this all worked out
> So help me to make it through
> I am confused, and I feel lost
> Thank you for being the type of God that can give me light
> When I feel surrounded by darkness
> I know that only you can keep me, because I can't keep myself
> My pain is great, But you my God is greater
> I love you, in Jesus name, Amen.

I curled up within the safety of Randy's arms knowing that God is going to have his way with me.

> "Therefore I tell you, do not worry about your life, what you will eat or drink; or about your body, what you will wear. Is

not life more important than food, and the body more important than clothes? Look at the birds of the air; they do not sow or reap or store away in barns, and yet your heavenly father feeds them. Are you not much more valuable than they? Who of you by worrying can add a single hour to his life?" (Matthew 6: 25-27)

The next morning Randy and I got up, and dressed for church without a single word spoken between us. His best friend Chris decided to attend church with us. Although I slept the entire night I felt totally drained and exhausted. Everything made my emotions stir up inside of me. I have always taken pride in the false sense of control I have had over my emotions. Where in the world had I misplaced my control today? While sitting in church the men of the dance ministry performed. I listened to the music, singing about God having a purpose, and burst into tears. I ran from the sanctuary. I could still hear the song as I stood in the basement hallway, head buried in my hands. My feelings at that moment were pain, confusion, and anger. I could feel God was working in his house, and better than that God was working on me. As I stood in the hall Reverend Johnson walked over, greeted me first with his usual hug, and declaration of love. He immediately noticed my tears and asked what was wrong. After I explained this was my first experience like this with my dad, and I wasn't sure I could endure any more like that. Rev. Johnson looked at me and said, "Everything is just as God would have it. Hold on and pray. I too will be praying for dad." He smiled at me and quietly continued on his path. Amazing, I thought to myself, God gives us just what we need when we need it.

> "Love must be sincere. Hate what is evil, cling to what is good. Be devoted to one another in brotherly love. Honor one another above yourselves. Never be lacking in zeal, but keep your spiritual fervor, serving the Lord. Be joyful in hope,

patient in affliction, faithful in prayer. Share with God's people who are in need. Practice hospitality." (Romans 12: 9-13)

I managed to compose myself long enough to make it back into the sanctuary. During the entire sermon I cried on Randy not even hearing what the minister was saying. I kept thinking to myself. I just don't understand. It hurt so bad, daddy not knowing me, what we have shared together my entire life just gone.

Randy decided to take Chris home after service. I cried the entire time. For the first time in my life the floodgates of my heart was completely open. Because of the way I looked we decided to pass on Sunday dinner at my parent's house. I lay in bed crying as silently as I could, while Randy quietly held me. Then he said, "Close your eyes while I pray."

> Heavenly Father, the creator of everything, we come before you humbly
> Thanking you Lord for another day, asking you Lord, to forgive us our trespasses
> As we forgive those who trespass against us, help us Lord, to deal with our situation
> Give my wife strength, I love and need her very much. Bless her parents Lord
> Help them to stay strong, bless the entire family as a whole, bless the sick and shut in
> Bless our Pastor and his family; bless the teachers and students of your word
> We love you Lord, as we know you love us, all these blessings we ask in the name of Jesus
> Amen.

The tone of his voice was so very soothing to me I dosed into a quiet slumber.

"Husbands, love your wives, just as Christ loved the church and gave himself up for her to make her holy, cleansing her by the washing with water through the word, and to present her to himself as a radiant church, without stain or wrinkle or any other blemish, but holy and blameless. In this same way, husbands ought to love their wives as their own bodies. He who loves his wife loves himself." (Ephesians 5: 25-28)

As the next few weeks passed daddy's episodes became more frequent, and more frustrating. It started wearing on everyone involved. Every time we tried to tell momma how to handle daddy she always said, "You just don't understand." Without any further explanation. I didn't even take into account maybe momma was tired. We couldn't even have a family discussion anymore without someone getting angry about something. Shamar told us he couldn't handle daddy being like this, so every time daddy had a problem with his memory Shamar would leave the house. After describing daddy's episodes to the doctor they explained it was time to evaluate daddy's condition. The only way of doing this was to take him into the emergency room and let them admit him into the hospital for evaluation. This process would take about a week. He would be kept on the psychiatric floor. We would only be able to see him a couple of hours on certain days of the week. They said momma would be able to visit him every day during meals. We needed to get a handle on what was happening to daddy, so as a family we agreed and decided to take him to the hospital the following day.

We all met at my parent's house the next evening. We explained to daddy that we were taking him to the hospital to be seen by the doctors. Daddy's mood was great. He was happy just to leave the house. This was the most cooperative daddy had been in what seemed a very long time. We sat in the emergency room for hours. After daddy's admission we had to wait for transportation to come and get him. As the hours passed daddy became agitated and wanted to go home. We kept rotating visitors so daddy wouldn't be too uneasy. Finally transportation came, that's when we started to question our decision. Daddy has never been away from home like this before. As they put him in the back of the ambulance it was no longer possible to hold back the tears. Daddy reassured everyone that everything was going to be okay. He smiled at us and was quite happy to be leaving. They were taking him to Saint Vincent's hospital, in Normandy, which was about forty-five minutes away from my house. We all cried together, Malcolm took momma home and I went home to get some rest.

The next day we were allowed to visit daddy. They allowed the entire family to see him. I didn't like how the doors were locked, but they couldn't afford to lose anyone including daddy. Once I entered the unit I saw daddy sitting in the common area. Daddy was looking very fragile, and fraile. When he saw me he smiled, "Eliana, how are you doing? What's going on with you?" My conversation with daddy was very pleasant and he seemed content. During our conversation he asked, "How did you get here, did you catch the bus?" I said, "No Daddy, I drove." He laughed with such surprise. "You drove, but you can't drive yet!" His remark tickled me. "Well, that part may be true, but I do have a license and a car." I started laughing too. During our conversation I realized daddy knew who I was just at a younger age. Because he was so happy to see me, and he remembered who I was, I didn't care what year it was for him. After a week at the hospital daddy was ready to go home, and we were all ready for daddy to come home. We spoke with the doctors during the course and they explained daddy wasn't eating well, and constantly tried to leave the unit. There were times when they had to restrain him. They said he is definitely in the stages of Alzheimer's disease, and will require special care and treatment from now on.

> "Children, obey your parents in the Lord, for this is right. Honor your father and mother—which is the first commandment with a promise—that it may go well with you and that you may enjoy long life on the earth. Fathers do not exasperate

your children instead, bring them up in the training and instruction of the Lord." (Ephesians 6: 1-4)

The day arrived when it was time for daddy to leave the hospital. Momma, Cadence, Raina, and I were there happy and very excited. Daddy was dressed and ready to go Momma had packed his belongings the night before so it was now time to leave. Momma signed the discharge papers and headed downstairs to get the car. We walked with daddy downstairs. As we approached the exit daddy stopped. He said, "I can't go out there." Raina who was holding daddy by the arm assured him, "Everything's okay daddy come on it's time to go." Daddy had such a look of fear in his face as he slowly pulled away from Raina. Cadence walked over and took daddy by his other arm trying to assure him that everything is fine and it was okay to leave the hospital. The closer daddy got to the exit his legs began to buckle. He was shaking badly, and could no longer stand on his own. We walked daddy back into the corridors of the hospital to sit down, and Raina went to call the doctor, while Cadence went outside to call Malcolm.

I tried to talk daddy into going outside. I tried to help daddy outside; I even tried to wheel him out in a wheelchair. He was petrified, and was not going through those doors. Shortly Raina returned and said the doctor would gladly come down and walk daddy out to the car. Seeing daddy this afraid was very disturbing to everyone. Malcolm arrived in what seemed to be no time and told daddy it was time to go. Once daddy saw Malcolm he seemed to relax and just walked to the car. Malcolm returned to his car and returned to work. The ride to their house was uneventful, and daddy was finally able to lie down in the comfort of his own home. Now it was time for another family meeting.

During the family meeting we had to come to some decisions about daddy's care. We could not spend the rest of our lives spending the night over here. The doctor gave us correspondence on Adult day care, and we just had to find the one that was best for daddy and momma. Tamera made the necessary arrangements, and daddy was to attend on Tuesday and Thursdays of every week. He was prescribed medicine to handle his agitation. Raina was in charge of his medicine. I created a logbook with a sign in sheet so we could monitor daddy's progress and behavior. Our trip to Georgia was already planned; most of us already purchased our tickets. We needed to get an approval from the doctor for daddy and everything else was a go. We agreed on visitation days, and after prayer we parted.

I spent the entire ride home in conversation with God, "I know there is a reason for this Lord, and I'm just not sure what. I feel like I'm lost in a wurl wind, not knowing what direction to go in. My job is driving me crazy, Randy is working the afternoon shift, I don't even see him anymore, and Dahlia is away at school. What am I supposed to be doing? Why must I be alone? My body feels like it doesn't even belong to me most of the time. I know I'm not in a position to question, but how about some guidance here. If this is a test, how about giving me my grade now." I felt God answer, "Do you really want your grade right now?" I answered, "No Lord, I just want some relief."

As I lay in bed I cried because I no longer had the drive within to continue at the pace which I was going. I committed to three days at my dad's house and I still had a husband and a home to take care of. My job was very demanding and they were depending on me too. I decided to read some scriptures and pray before going to sleep. Why does Randy have to be gone when I need him the most?

> "Then he said to them all; "If anyone would come after me, he must deny himself and take up his cross daily and follow me. For whoever wants to save his life will lose it, but whoever loses his life for me will save it. What good is it for a man to gain the whole world, and yet lose or forfeit his very self? (Luke 9: 23-25)

CHAPTER 5

Expect the Unexpected

WE KEPT OUR scheduled days and dealt with daddy's condition accordingly. Even Shamar managed to put his emotions aside long enough to participate. I could feel my body giving way to the tiredness more every day. We kept telling daddy he was going home soon and that seemed to keep him happy.

One Saturday afternoon Randy and I decided to visit my parents. During our drive over, while sitting at a red light we were involved in a car accident. She didn't notice the light was red, and although she wasn't traveling at a high rate of speed she pushed our car into the van which was in front of us. She was very apologetic, and we understood that's why they call them accidents. We exchanged information and agreed to file a police report. The rear of the car was smashed, however drivable so we continued on our way. While I sat in my parents kitchen I could feel my head throbbing, and my vision was blurred. After we left the police station, Randy and I drove to the hospital to be thoroughly checked out. They gave me something for pain and stiffness, and told me to follow up with my personal physician and sent us on our way.

As I lay in bed I could feel the room spinning uncontrollably. To close my eyes made things worse. I rose from bed thinking I could just walk it off, and couldn't keep my balance. I fell to the floor thinking to myself not what. The spinning was so bad I started to vomit.

Once again it was time to visit my doctor. Dr. Vang wasn't available, so I agreed to see one of the other physicians. After my exam he told me, "You have vertigo" which is normally caused by an inner ear infection. I didn't have an infection, but it can also be caused by head trauma. My recent car accident seemed to be the culprit. We were leaving for Georgia in five days and I was not going to let anything disrupt that.

After consulting with daddy's doctor we were given the okay to travel with caution. Daddy and Momma left Friday morning with Raina, her husband Matthew, Malcolm, Cadence, and Wade. Randy was scheduled to work Friday, so we left Saturday morning. The weather was beautiful, the temperature was perfect. We were taking a much needed vacation with the company of my family. Malcolm met us in the lobby of the hotel, "Guess who's here?" Before I could answer there stood my Uncle Parker. I hadn't seen Uncle Parker since I was about fifteen years old. I was so very happy to see him. Malcolm said we were going to Grandma's house in a little while, so we rushed upstairs to put our things away, and tell everyone we made it safely.

The house that grandma lived in was the same house daddy grew up in. Grand daddy owned the property and when de died he was buried in the cemetery right down the street. When you live in the northern states everything is very different. Small towns are just that, country roads, unpaved streets, everybody knows everyone, and when a stranger arrives everyone celebrates. I told Randy I wanted to go to the cemetery and find my grandfather's gravesite, because I had never been there before. Momma and daddy never discussed much about their childhood. Sometimes because of all the things they had to endure just to give us a better life, they would much rather forget. In grandma's backyard stood multiple pecan trees, peat moss was everywhere. Daddy seemed happy to be there at first, but later seemed withdrawn. I couldn't be sure but I don't think he remembered Parker. Daddy had already left home by the time Uncle Parker was born.

We had a wonderful barbeque dinner at Grandma's house. Randy and I sat and had a long conversation with grandma. We looked at pictures and gathered history. Grandma told me exactly where the cemetery that grand daddy was buried. "Right down the road, just beyond the church where we were both members." Grandma said she still attends church when her health permits. We asked grandma how old she was, but for the fifth year in a row she replied, "eighty-five."

After awhile daddy was uncomfortable and wanted to return to the hotel. Malcolm was driving them, so we all decided to let grandma get some rest, and return the next day. Randy and I decided to attend my grandparent's church in the morning. I was so excited and happy. "Thank you Lord for this wonderful family reunion." Thank God trouble doesn't last always.

> "Listen to your father, who gave you life, and do not despise your mother when she is old. Buy the truth and do not sell it, get wisdom, discipline and understanding. The father of a righteous man has great joy; he who has a wise son delights in him. May your father and mother be glad; may she who gave you birth rejoice." (Proverbs 23: 22-25)

That Sunday morning Randy and I dressed and drove to Greater Mt. Pleasant Baptist Church. They parked on the lawn everywhere. Everyone was so friendly, and knew who we belonged to. I loved the feeling of comfort they provided, and would like to model my behavior towards greeting strangers in the church after them.

After service it was time to drive to the cemetery, which was actually one country mile. I had never been to this cemetery before and grandma didn't remember where grand daddy's plot was, so we were on our own. We parked at the front gate and split up. I walked until I couldn't see Randy, reading every tombstone I saw. Some of the tombstones were hand written, I was looking at history. I was amazed by the way everything is in the south. The graves are not underground, the top of the crypts are above the surface. You really had to walk around the graves. There were ravens sitting on some of the tombstones, and I thought to myself, this looks like something out of a movie. Randy and I met up half way and he also could not find grand daddy's plot. After about an hour we decided to give up. We returned to the car disappointed, and as Randy turned the car around I shouted, "Stop the car now!" I got out and walked directly to a grave that was sectioned off with bricks. There was room for four graves, but one crypt was present. The others were vacant; as I looked at the tombstone I could not believe my eyes.

Parker McCoy Sr.
Feb. 10, 1904
Oct. 18, 1974
Now Cometh Eternal Rest

    I found my grand fathers grave. I decided at that moment I wanted to know the history of where I came from. I wanted to know everything about the lives of my family. After taking pictures it was time to go to grandma's house.

    By the time we reached grandma's house there were people everywhere. I was afraid something was wrong. Then I saw Grandma was sitting on the porch, and everyone from the church was there visiting. They apologized for neglecting her by not visiting, and told her because we were there for service they were reminded of their responsibility to a shut in member. Just think God sent us all the way here to remind a congregation about a forgotten member.

    We went back to the hotel so I could get some rest. I was having the time of my life, but my body was still very tired. Once I laid down the room started to spin. I became sick to my stomach and couldn't be still. I started to cry, because I just couldn't understand how this could happen so suddenly. The rest of the day I spent in our hotel room. No more fun activities today just rest.

    Early the next morning we headed off to St. Augustine for some sightseeing. Although I continued to feel dizzy, I was able to get around. This was the second best vacation ever, unable to compare to the trip Randy and I took to California a few years back. The sights were beautiful, and we spent a lot of time bonding.

After viewing the sights in St. Augustine, we drove back to the hotel so I could get some rest. I was feeling a little sick from the constant dizziness, and just wanted to lie down. The rest of our vacation was calm and very quiet. We were able to spend some quality time with Uncle Parker, and Aunt Rose. Although I didn't feel well, in my heart I was rejoicing.

We returned home glad to see the house was still standing. We left Dahlia whom was home from school for the summer in the house. I was a little nervous, but as usual Dahlia didn't let me down.

Although daddy's condition didn't worsen, his episodes were still quite frequent. I was emotionally adjusting, but still grieving for my loss. Things were still hectic at work, but I thank God for Patrick. His wisdom allowed me to receive good sound advice. Patrick seemed to fill in for my dad. Cain and I worked together since I was twenty-two years old, and our relationship was full of many ups and downs. Although he did not inherit his father's understanding, he tried to offer a listening ear sometimes.

Once the vertigo subsided I was able to maintain more of a normal life. Work, home, bible study, my parents, I started asking God for a change in my life.

> Dear Lord, Thank you for today
> Guide me, speak to my heart
> Bless me to understand your word, Keep my family safe
> May my actions glorify your name, Change me Lord, I love you
> Forgive me for not consulting you, earlier in my life
> Bless those who need and want you, bless me to reach them
> May all who see me, see you, Amen.

The seasons started to change, and so did daddy's behavior. Through my research I learned the sunlight played a very important factor with daddy's condition. The hallucinations daddy was experiencing were caused by a malfunction of his sleep wake cycle in his brain. When you are sleeping you brain allows your subconscious to work. When you wake your brain tells your subconscious to stop and your brain functions from your conscious mind takes over. In other words you know you are awake. When the sleep wake cycle isn't working, you brain doesn't give the signal that you are awake. Therefore you are still dreaming, although you are physically awake. The exposure to the sunlight will reset the sleep wake cycle, when the season changes there is less sunlight available. That makes things a little tough. Although your sleep wake cycle is not the only thing affected by sunlight. We needed to keep daddy busy. The adult day care center was working well, daddy thought he was back to work.

꩜꩜꩜

I was completing my payroll, and my telephone rang. It was Raina, "How ya doing Eliana? I'm okay, just frustrated trying to deal with Raymond and his father." Raymond was doing poorly in school, and may not graduate. Raymond is a gifted child; working with numbers came naturally. He has a photographic memory. He was offered many scholarships to schools like Cambridge and Westwood when he was younger, he refused to attend; he said if I made him go he would run away, because he would not be able to see his dad if he went away to school. All of Raymond's test scores were off the charts, and he took his S.A.T.'s when he was thirteen years old. Once he moved in with his dad he wasn't forced to do many things. Raymond started doing poorly in school, and because of the terrible communication I had with his father, and my bitterness towards Raymond, I did nothing.

Raina said to me, "I can't believe you are still angry. That is your only son and you can't just give up on him. All of our children have grown up to be productive and Raymond will too with your help and guidance. You have to step up and do the right thing." At that moment I realized she was right. I had let Raymond down. I needed to forgive them, so God could forgive me. "Raina, you are absolutely right, and what better time to make a change than right now." I hung up the phone and started to cry. I needed to let go of the past, my pain, and all of my anger. Raymond was still a child, my son, I love him so much, but my pain was so deep. I asked God to help me release what I would not let go of on my own. I cried four years of anger away in one afternoon.

> "For if you forgive men when they sin against you, your heavenly father will also forgive you. But if you do not forgive men their sins, your father will not forgive your sins." (Matthew 6: 14-15)

I picked up the phone and called Raymond's father, "Hey Ray, this is Eliana, don't speak, I just need to share something with you. I want you to know I'm very sorry for everything that I have ever done that may have hurt you. Don't misunderstand I am not sorry for the outcome of my life, just the pain my actions may have caused you. I want to be there for Raymond, and I know he needs me too." He said quietly, "I accept your apology Eliana." I hung up the phone and waited for Raymond to get home from school.

Later that afternoon, once I was sure Raymond was home, I called his dad's house. My conversation with Raymond was brief and to the point. "Baby I love you, and I have been very angry with you and your dad about the way you left home. I want you to know I'm not angry any more, and I want you to know that I'm here for you no matter what. You have to start doing right by yourself. Life is too short to start out making terrible mistakes. I have made enough for the both of us. Randy and I love you, and want to be an active part of your life if you will let us. I look forward to seeing you on the weekend, and we will talk more from now on." Raymond said, "I love you too momma." We hung up the phone and I thanked God for giving me one more chance.

Things were less hectic after that, and my job performance was improving. Randy was up for a transfer to the day shift soon, and Dahlia was home. Daddy's condition was stable, and life is good.

"This is the day the Lord has made; let us rejoice and be glad in it." (Psalm 118 24)

During a training session with our computer software support company I was called from training for an emergency phone call. It was momma, "Eliana I need you to sit down." Every time the phone rang and it was family I was afraid something was wrong with daddy. I quickly responded, "What's wrong with daddy? It's not your father, she said. I don't know if you have heard yet, but there was a bad car accident; Sylvia and Lacey were in the car." I could feel my heart sink. Lacey is my God daughter and Sylvia is her mother. "Is Sylvia okay? I asked, No Eliana she was killed." The only thing I could think of at that point was Lacey; I needed to get to her, pick her up and hold her. I needed to let her know that everything was going to be alright. "Where is Lacey momma? She was in the car with Sylvia. What hospital, I need to get there right away." After what seemed like an eternity momma answered, "Eliana she didn't make it. " I couldn't comprehend what she was saying. "What do you mean she didn't make it, Lacey didn't make it where. Momma please, where is she? Eliana, she died this morning at the scene." I sat down in my chair staring at the picture of Lacey on my desk. When Lacey was born she became like one of my children, spending much time with us, even traveling on our family vacations. I spent the rest of the afternoon in the training session not paying attention to anything being said, I then went to Sylvia's mother house to find out what happened.

Once I arrived at the house I entered the room where Sylvia's mom was sitting. One look into her eyes told me everything was true, Sylvia and Lacey were dead. Apparently a man driving over ninety miles per hour ran a red light, while Sylvia and lacey were driving home. The impact killed Sylvia immediately Lacey died at the scene. We held each other and cried.

Margaret explained she was having them cremated, because she could not make herself bury them. I told her I needed to see lacey for myself, because I needed closure. The family decided to allow viewing for closure purposes. Sylvia's body was in too bad of shape to be viewed, but Lacey was prepared. Dahlia and Raymond accompanied me to the funeral home. I slowly walked up to Lacey's casket ready to gain closure. I looked at her body, knowing she wasn't present, but feeling a need to speak anyway. "Lacey I know this is only the house God chose for you to occupy, and now you are resting in peace. I look forward to seeing you again one day with our father."

> Dear Lord, humbly I come before you, thanking you for
> The life which you allowed to touch mine
> Give her family strength, Bless me with your words of wisdom
> And provide her family with comfort. I love you Lord, and thank you
> For loving me. Amen.

I left the funeral home broken hearted, but knowing I would understand it better by and by.

"Remember him—Before the silver cord is severed or the golden bowl is broken; before the pitcher is shattered at the spring, or the wheel broken at the well, and the dust returns to the ground it came from, and the spirit returns to God who gave it." (Ecclesiastes 12: 6-7)

The memorial service was nice. Sylvia and Lacey's memorial was full of life, love and happiness. I remembered two weeks prior I saw lacey at the movies with her friends. She ran to me, gave me a big hug and told me how she missed me. I told her I loved her, and to come and spend some time with us soon. I had no idea that would be the last time I would see her alive. I was glad God allowed me one more hug and kiss before she left.

Daddy's doctor visits were every three months. I volunteered to take them. It was my opportunity to spend more time with daddy, and a chance to take them to lunch. I was feeling sick quite often for what seem to be no apparent reason. Although I continued to go to work daily, I felt I just couldn't function. God gave me relief within my personal life, but my professional life was falling apart.

Cain constantly threatened my position with demotion, and it seemed every time there was a crisis in my life, he was right there to turn the screws. I would start my day with him in my office fussing about things that I wasn't even responsible for and the day would end with him fussing at me. I felt he gained pleasure in treating me bad. My emotions were getting the best of me.

I would meet with Patrick about things going on, and he would schedule meetings with Cain and me to discuss our differences. I didn't neglect any of my work, everything was always on time, however I did complete a lot of work from home. Cain would look at me and say, "Patrick is old school, and we need to do things differently." Cain explained to me the way Patrick does things is obsolete, and I am a part of what is obsolete. When I first hired into the company I worked under a store manager. After a couple of years I was promoted to store manager, at that point I worked directly under Cain. After a year I took a reduction in pay to transfer to their main office, and I started working directly for Patrick. Through the course of years I learned to accommodate Patrick's needs, and although Cain and I worked together Patrick was still running the company. After eleven years of formatting a certain order of things, Cain told me from now on he was running the business, making the business decisions, and I was to answer to him. Now I have never had a problem with authority, Patrick was still working in the office everyday still making decisions, a predicament I was not prepared to deal with. Patrick would request things, and Cain would come behind him fussing at me because I didn't do what he wanted first.

According to everything I was aware of, Patrick was ultimately still running the business, and simply preparing Cain to one day take over so Patrick could finally retire. I finally reached a point when Cain would come to me with his daily attitude I would tell him, "you need to speak to your father, and after the two of you work it out, please tell me what you want from me and it will be done." Through my many meetings with Cain I could tell he felt I didn't respect him the way I should. It was apparent Cain wanted to replace me. When I talked to Patrick about it he gave me this explanation.

"Any time there is a new administration, they bring in their own people. I don't plan on being here forever, and I am trying to slowly hand the business to Cain. Soon Cain will be running the business as he sees fit, and it will be necessary for everyone to work together on the same page." I understood Patrick's point, but based on everything Patrick taught me about business I wanted to let him know some of Cain's business decisions were not very wise. My job has always consisted of many duties. Keeping the company within regulation was one of them. There were times when Cain was not aware because he didn't deal with issues first hand. I felt his decisions weren't wise and I would argue and refuse to cooperate because I felt it wasn't the best decision. I would tell him why he couldn't do what he wanted. I guess that wasn't wise on my behalf.

> "Everyone must submit himself to the governing authorities, for there is no authority except that which God has established. The authorities that exist have been established by God. Consequently, he who rebels against the authority is rebelling against what God has instituted, and those who do so will bring judgment on themselves." (Romans 13: 1-2)

My administrative assistant was leaving, and it was necessary for me to hire someone. Because of my many obligations, Cain wanted us to hire someone qualified to take over my position if necessary. I prayed about the entire situation, and placed an ad in the newspaper.

> Dear Lord, thank you for today, you are a God of all answers
> You have a situation all worked out, before I even know there
>   is a problem

> Help me to find the right person, for this job, send someone;
> that knows you Lord
> Help me to be a better person, bless me with understanding
> and wisdom
> Help me to be bold when it comes to you Lord
> May your word live in my heart always
> I love you Lord, Amen.

I made time to pray before and after every interview, and when I met Tabitha I knew she was the one. I explained to her Cain's desire to replace me one day, and I was more than willing to teach her everything she needed to know to operate the office efficiently. I could feel the word of God seeping from my pores. She was experiencing a personal crisis, and I was more than happy to explain what God's word said about living.

I would come in every Thursday morning telling her what I learned in bible study the night before. Sometimes I would spend the entire day talking about God and his goodness while working. It seemed to relieve my pressure with Cain. I was always told religion and work should never mix, but I could no longer hold my tongue. If my belief and love for God was in me, then it should radiate from my entire being. Tabatha would work out to be the perfect replacement. Although they did not want me to leave the company, only step down from my present position, I didn't think it would be fair to the company or me if I stayed.

I considered leaving for many years, and every time I thought I would leave I would have one of those talks with Patrick. He always told me he didn't want me to leave, and that I didn't have to go. I realized my only reason for not leaving was Patrick. Over the many years I developed such a bond with him. I love Patrick; he has always been there for me. More like a surrogate father than a boss. I would go above and beyond for him. My problem was I didn't have the same feelings for his son. Cain and I were close for a very long time, and although I blamed him for the dissolution of our friendship I was the one that changed.

Once I re-established my relationship with God the Holy Spirit awakened within me. This manifestation brought upon a change in my entire personality. No human can determine the degree or the rate of change, but sure as you are born you will change.

"On that day you will realize that I am in my father, and you are in me, and I am in you. Whoever has my commands and obeys them, he is the one who loves me. He who loves me will be loved by my father, and I too will love him and show myself to him." (John 14: 20-21)

As time passed I no longer concerned myself at work with friendship. My concern was getting my job done to the best of my ability. There is right and there is wrong, and you were one or the other. I was fair in dealing with all of the employees, but when you deal with a group of people someone is always going to be unhappy. My goal was not to please, but whatever was in the best interest of the company. I never had an issue with what people would say, and during new employee orientations I would explain that we are not here to make friends; we are here to complete a task for monetary consideration. However if anyone came to me with a problem I would give him or her proper resources, and a quick lesson in faith.

The closer my relationship with God, the harder my workday became. I would leave at the end of the day frustrated, drained and hurt. I sometimes felt like a moving target in a shooting gallery. I continued to frequent Dr. Vang's office with my health issues, and Randy and I continued to pray.

CHAPTER 6

Not My Job!

WE WERE STILL waiting for Randy's transfer to days to come through. He was scheduled to start his new position after returning from vacation. I was so excited that he would be working the same hours as I. It had been a very tough year. I was now having conversations with Raymond about problems he felt he was having with his dad. I was objective when I spoke to the children about him, regardless to the type of person I felt he was, they would learn and decide for themselves who he was and the type of relationship they would have with him, besides he wasn't all bad; we married, had children and he was always an excellent provider when it came to our family as a unit.

    I found myself at work fighting back tears on a regular basis. I wasn't being informed about meetings. Changes were being made that I wasn't aware of. I was slowly being eliminated from the office. Conversations would cease when I entered the room; this was very personal. I was very surprised Cain and Tabatha would behave this way, but we both knew I would have to leave of my own will. I would cry all the way home from work as the days became unbearable. After prayer I would talk to Randy about it. He would tell me to be strong, "They just want to break your spirit." I would leave in the morning headed for work, and by the time I arrived I would have a massive headache. I continued to do my duties working around everyone. I refused to cry in anyone's presence, and I wouldn't get angry with anyone either. I knew this was the course chosen for me and I know trouble doesn't last always. I found myself quoting scriptures and praying in my office a lot. When Cain would call me into his office I would take a moment to pray first, asking God to give me the right words. No matter what happened I was not going to make God look bad. Not a word was spoken unless someone needed a question answered.

> "Therefore, since we have been justified through faith, we have peace with God through our Lord Jesus Christ, through whom we have gained access by faith into this grace in which we now stand. And we rejoice in the hope of the glory of God. Not only so, but we also rejoice in our sufferings, because we know that suffering produces perseverance, perseverance, character; and character hope. And hope does not disappoint us, because God has poured out his love into our hearts by the Holy Spirit, whom he has given us." (Romans 5: 1-5)

I started to notice the employees were no longer calling me for anything. Anytime anything was needed everyone was directed to Tabitha. Cain, Tabitha, and Eugene, our general manager seemed to be having a lot of fun with this. I guess they should have, because they were the cause of my misery. Finally Cain called me into his office for the big conference.

Apparently Cain and Eugene collected letters from the employees regarding their personal feelings towards me. Cain always told me I needed to be more, "warm and fuzzy" some of the employees felt I had a non caring attitude, I spoke impersonally, wasn't friendly or nice. I was too direct and business like, for them to enjoy my presence. Cain read the letters to me with pleasure. Although some of the things said hurt my feelings, I refused to show any emotions. As he read the letters he would look at me and tell me how unacceptable this was. "The guys just don't like you" he said with a smirk on his face. I thought to myself, if the letters had been written by good standing, long term employees I think I would have been a little more understanding. The letters were written by employees that were fired, or involved in some form of litigation with the company, or the employee was new. Their complaints were petty, and I could have named legitimate problems with each person involved including those working in the office. I was insulted by the remarks, but closed my eyes and prayed while Cain continued to read.

> Heavenly Father, Protect my heart
> Forgive me for my anger, Hold my tongue
> So I won't say anything displeasing to you, Encircle me with your word
> Bless this man with peace; Let him feel your presence in this room
> I love you Lord, Amen.

When Cain finished the last letter he explained to me if I didn't change he would have to change things himself. Tabitha was more of a people pleasing person, you do the math. Once I left Cain's office there was silence among everyone the rest of the day. I thought to myself there will come a day when you'll miss my presence.

> "But I tell you who hear me; Love your enemies, do good to those who hate you, bless those who curse you, pray for those who mistreat you. If someone strikes you on one cheek, turn to him the other also. If someone takes your cloak, do not stop him from taking your tunic. Give to everyone who asks you, and if anyone takes what belong to you, do not demand it back. Do to others as you would have them do to you." (Luke 6: 27-31)

Two weeks later I was once again sitting in Cain's office. I could tell it wasn't going to be good because Tabitha and Eugene left the building. Cain started by saying, "You know this isn't working the way things are right now. You don't seem to be happy to be here anymore, and I am no longer happy with your performance. I have to be here, this is my life and there is nowhere else for me to go. I can't do anything else, but you don't have to be here, this is not your life. I just don't think this is for you anymore." Finally I could no longer contain my emotions. Tears were running down my cheeks as Cain spoke to me. Once he noticed the tears his tone became soft. "What I'm saying is you don't have to leave the office, just take a different position with hourly pay. Your schedule can be flexible and then you can take care of your dad. You have so many things going on in your life, and this way you can still be around to help out." Then he asked me, "Are you crying because of this?" I closed my eyes asking God to help me and then replied, "Your right Cain, this probably isn't for me anymore." I could tell by Cain's expression although breaking me made him very happy, this was not the response he was looking for. His tone changed, "If you leave where would you go? What would you do? Don't answer right away, just think about it, talk it over with Randy, and we can discuss things in about a week." The entire tone of the office changed. Everything seemed back to normal. At that moment I realized when you cut off your nose to spite your face, you only get to see what you can't smell anymore.

    I went home and explained to Randy everything that was said earlier that day. Randy held me while I cried, and then we prayed.

> Dear Lord, We come before you humbly
> Asking that you guide us in the direction you want us to go
> Forgive us for being disobedient, have you way with us
> We are at a crossroad Lord; tell us through your word what you will have us to do
> Give us comfort and strength; bless everyone at the office with understanding
> We love and adore you Lord
> In Jesus name, Amen.

Then we started reading scriptures in search of our answers from God.

"May your unfailing love come to me, O Lord, your salvation according to your promise, then I will answer the one who taunts me, for I trust in your word. Do not snatch the word of truth from my mouth, for I have put my hope in your laws. I will always obey your law, forever and ever. I will walk about in freedom, for I have sought out your precepts. I will speak of your statutes before kings and will not be put to shame, for I delight in your commands because I love them. I lift up my hands to your commands, which I love, and I meditate on your decrees." (Psalm 119: 41-48)

After a couple of days I requested a conference with Cain. He, Tabitha and Eugene were overly nice. Although I was beginning to enjoy this, it was now time to put my professional life in order. Cain looked at me as though he knew what I was going to say so I started the conversation. "Cain I want to start by saying how much I really appreciate you and your father. I came here seventeen years ago and fell in love with everything about this place, but I no longer have the drive necessary to continue." Cain sat there looking at me in shock. "Did you talk to Randy about this? What did he say? What are you going to do if you're not working? Do you have another job lined up?" Before I could answer any one question Cain was asking another. "Yes Cain, I talked to Randy, and he supports whatever I need and want. I don't know what I'll do, but I need to allow growth here as well as in my own life."

So the decision was made, negotiations were complete, preparations were in motion. To Cain's surprise it wasn't some ploy to make him grovel, although I felt he got what he wanted. Daddy always said, "Be careful what you ask for, you just might get it." I spent the next few weeks cleaning, moving things and reorganizing what used to be my office for my replacement. Everyone seemed a little distraught by the knowledge of my departure, but a weight was lifted from me. Cain even asked that I don't tell anyone in the company I was leaving. I was happy at work and at home, thank you Lord.

Randy and I were outside planting flowers before leaving for bible study. I could feel numbness in my toes as though my feet were really cold. I wasn't sure what was wrong, so I went into the house, took off my sandals, put on a pair of socks and shoes, and resumed what I was doing.

As the days passed the numbness moved from just my toes to my entire foot. I made a doctor's appointment to find out just what was going on with my body. Dr. Vang said they needed to test me for diabetes. She also said a B-12 deficiency would also cause my feet to go completely numb. I went home very uncomfortable and upset. Walking around is hard when you don't have feeling in your feet. There is an annoying kind of pain that's always present.

Two days later during lunch I decided to walk to the store for snacks. The gas station was just across the street. I purchased my snacks and headed back to the office. I notice pain that went from the lower part of my back down to my feet. With each step the pain was worse. I needed to get back to my office where I could sit, maybe put my feet up hoping the pain would stop. After a while the pain went away. I didn't know what caused it, but I didn't want to feel that again. The pain finally subsided to my relief, but shortly after it returned worse than before. I could barely walk. I had one of the guys help me to my car and drove to the hospital praying all the way.

By the time I was seen by the doctor in the emergency room, the spasms had stopped, but the numbness and pain was all the way up to my knees. The doctors tested me for everything they could think of, but every test came back normal. I started to cry because I knew exactly what I was feeling, and I was growing very weary. The emergency room doctor referred me to neurology. I made my appointment and took the medicine prescribed to control the pain.

The next day I felt I was better so off to work I went. During the day the spasms returned. The spasms felt like electrical currents running from my legs through my back. All I could do was cry, Patrick told me to go home and get some rest. I think he felt stress was the culprit. I couldn't walk, so Tabitha called Dahlia. Randy Jr. agreed to meet us at my house, and Tabitha agreed to drive me home. When I arrived Randy Jr. was there waiting to take me to the hospital, but I only wanted to lie down.

The day of my doctor's appointment was finally here. Getting around was very difficult these days, but I managed without having to explain to anyone at work what was wrong. I have always been very open about my feelings when it comes to my personal life, it's just that personal. I never believed anybody except Patrick cared anyway. That Monday I was completing some of my daily duties when I went down stairs to get some supplies. My legs gave out, and I had to grab on to the counter to keep from falling. The pain was so intense I started to cry. Eugene and Patrick helped me back up the stairs to my office. Patrick had a look of great concern on his face. "What's going on with you Eliana?" I started to cry, "I just don't know Patrick; I have an appointment with the neurologist this afternoon and hope to get some answers then. Go Now!" Patrick said, "Just leave everything as it is, it will all be here when you get back." Once the pain started to subside I drove myself to the hospital to see the neurologist, and to find some answers.

> Dear Lord, I don't know what's wrong with me
> But I know that you are having your way
> Thank you for being the kind of God that has solutions, just
>   beyond what I may think is a problem
> Thank you for loving me, better than I love myself
> Have your way with me Lord, I'm ready
> I surrender all to you Lord
> Amen.

During the consultation with Dr. Ore I became very discouraged. It appeared everything was visibly normal. Finally I snapped, "I am tired of funding the entire medical profession. I have been going back and forth to doctors and no one can seem to find anything wrong. Although I would like to believe that I have finally lost my mind, it has occurred to me that my sanity should not be in question here." Dr. Ore asked me to have a little more patience and she would be right back. Once she returned I apologized for my outburst, she was catching the brunt of all the previous appointments I had experienced. She took out her instruments to check my reflexes. As she checked each joint in my leg even I noticed there was no response. After my exam she called in another physician to check, still no response. Then she said, "We need to admit you right now so we can perform an MRI. MRI stands for Magnetic Resonance Imaging. A relatively new form of imaging that produces precise and highly detailed pictures of the brain and spinal cord.

Once all the admission papers were filled out and approved I was taken to my room, shortly after I was taken for my first series of test. The following morning I was visited by a team of neurologist. They explained the MRI of the brain wasn't conclusive, so they weren't sure exactly what the problem was, but needed to perform an MRI of my spine. I f they didn't get all the answers they needed from that they would have to do a lumbar puncture better known as a spinal tap, and a cat scan (computerized axial tomography) which uses x-rays to produce images of the central nervous system. I was thankful Randy and my family was there by my side.

After the test Dr. Logan came to me and told me they were sending a social worker up to my room to visit. This action told me right away that there was something really wrong. I asked her, "What's wrong with me?" She looked at me and said, "Well we need to do that spinal tap we discussed earlier to be sure, but it looks like multiple sclerosis. If that is the diagnosis you will be put on steroids for a period of time and we will move forward from there." After Dr. Logan left, the social worker came into my room. She wanted to know who I lived with, my sleeping arrangements, stairs involved in the home and locations of bathrooms. I was puzzled because I didn't feel that bad. After she left the room two gentlemen came in. They said they were from physical and occupational therapy. They needed to see if I could walk, and get around on my own. After spending some time with them they told me I would be okay at home with Randy and Dahlia there. I went to sleep thanking God for keeping mere here one more day. The next morning when I woke I prayed, read my scriptures and waited to see my doctor.

> "But he said to me, my grace is sufficient for you, for my power is made perfect in weakness. Therefore I will boast all the more gladly about my weaknesses, so that Christ's power may rest on me. That is why, for Christ's sake, I delight in weaknesses, in insults, in hardships, in persecutions, in difficulties. For when I am weak, then I am strong." (2 Corinthians 12: 9-19)

Dr. Logan returned to perform the lumbar puncture. I was glad, because God allowed me to see another day. Today was my birthday and I knew great things were going to come from this experience. Later in the afternoon the neurology team came into my room for a consultation. They took me to a section which had computer monitors and x-ray screens. Dr. Logan began to speak, "This is the MRI of your brain, and this is the MRI of your spine. As you can see what looks like spots are lesions. In the brain and spinal cord there are cells called neurons that transmit signals within the central nervous system and other parts of the body. These signals control our physical functions and thinking abilities. Signals pass through neurons by way of nerve fibers called axons. For protection, axons are surrounded by a covering called myelin. In multiple sclerosis, myelin becomes damaged, and consequently axons lose some of their protective covering. Although it is not understood why this happens, MS is believed to start when environmental and /or genetic factors trigger a person's immune system to inappropriately attack myelin. The body's own white blood cells break down myelin, causing inflammation, or swelling, around the nerve tissue. Inflammation can clear up on its own so that the affected areas of the central nervous system recover partially or completely. But if inflammation is severe, lasts a long time, or occurs repeatedly in the same place, then the myelin can become permanently damaged, leaving the axons exposed. This permanent loss of myelin is called demyelization. Demyelization causes scarring or hardening (sclerosis) of areas in the brain and spinal cord. On MRI's multiple areas of scarring or hardening in the central nervous system tissue are often seen, thus the name Multiple Sclerosis. These hardened areas interfere with the transmission of signals along the axons in the central nervous system, causing problems with motor (physical movement), sensory, and thinking skills.

After I was given a few moments to absorb what I was being told Dr. Logan reviewed my medical charts with me. She could coincide past problems with the location of lesions on my brain, or spine. Strange enough I was overcome with relief. I haven't lost my mind; it wasn't my imagination, "Thank you Jesus for giving me peace within my troubles."

Once I returned to my room I called Randy at work to inform him what the doctor said. "Are you okay Eliana?" he asked with such calmness in his voice. "I'm really okay; as a matter of fact I feel better knowing that I still have my sanity." Randy promised to be there as soon as possible and I proceeded to call Dahlia.

Once Dahlia arrived, I told her to sit down so I could explain what was going on with my body. Dahlia sat, but would not take her eyes off my eyes. She had a look of concern, but I could detect God's strength within her. "Listen to me very carefully; after all of the test the doctors have come up with a diagnosis. They told me I have multiple sclerosis." Dahlia continued to stare into my eyes. "I don't know where my life will go from here, but I thank God it wasn't something worse. Are you okay momma? Dahlia asked without taking her eyes off of me. "I'm okay," I responded. "Why are you staring at me like that? It is almost like you are looking for something else. I'm looking into your eyes momma, because if you weren't okay I would see it, but since you are okay I know that I will be okay. As long as you hold it together I know I can handle things. If one tear had fallen while you were talking to me I would have fallen apart." Dahlia gave me a big hug, and while she held me she whispered in my ear, "I am going to help you with anything I can. I love you momma. I love you too baby." We then started watching the television in silence.

> "For this reason I kneel before the father, from whom his whole family in heaven and on earth derives its name. I pray that out of his glorious riches he may strengthen you with power through his spirit in your inner being. So that Christ may dwell in your hearts through faith. And I pray that you, being rooted and established in love, may have power, together with all the saints, to grasp how wide and long and high and deep is the love of Christ, and to know this love that surpasses knowledge—That you may be filled to the measure of all the fullness of God. (Ephesians 3: 14-19)

After telling Randy and Dahlia what was going on with me I felt a relief. I called Randy Jr. and his wife Nadia. They immediately came to the hospital. Rand and Nadia offered much love and support. They agreed to help with anything and everything I needed now or in the future. I celebrated my birthday with my entire family knowing that finally I am on God's program.

> Dear Lord,
> Thank you for being so patient with me
> Forgive me for my disobedience with you
> You have blessed me with strength, courage and knowledge
> You surrounded me with your love and kindness
> You have blessed me with direction
> I trust you; knowing in all things you are able
> Thank you for being God all by yourself
> I love you Lord, and feel your love towards me
> Amen.

Anxious to return home I knew my life would never be the same. The thought of a new life with God was very exciting for me. I realized it was time to give what God has given me. The day I returned home from the hospital my entire family was there. Tamera and Raina prepared dinner, and we had a marvelous time together. Once everyone went home it was time for bed. Although I was glad to be home my challenges were just beginning. I needed help with just about everything. Because Daddy has Alzheimer's I decided not to tell Momma about my condition just yet. I also didn't want anyone outside of my family to know. I just wasn't ready yet. My days of recovery were very difficult at first. I couldn't walk distances, my balance was bad, and I was having muscle spasms that wouldn't allow me to stand sometimes. I found myself crying a lot when I was alone. I felt like I lost something. I wanted to do everything for myself, and didn't like asking for help. Randy drove me everywhere I wanted or needed to go. If he wasn't at work he was right by my side. I love him for being so supportive, but he started treating me like I was breakable.

"Now faith is being sure of what we hope for and certain of what we do not see. This is what the ancients were commended for. By faith we understand that the universe was formed at God's command, so that what is seen was not made out of what was visible." (Hebrews 11: 1-3)

I felt a need to live as normal as I could. My problem was how to live a normal life with a life that is no longer normal. I needed to re-examine myself. I started to learn my limitations, not pushing myself beyond my limit. We should all learn our limitations in life.

As time passed, I started to adjust to my physical disabilities, but my emotional state of mind was questionable. There are therapies, and treatment available, but no known cure. The medication will slow the progression, but would not stop any relapses. I would have to have an injection weekly with no guarantees. Randy, Raina and Randy Jr. volunteered to give me my injections, because I have a fainting fear of needles. They went with me for training, and the therapy began. Side effects to the injection were explained, be we had no clue as to what we were really in for. Severe flu like symptoms is putting things lightly. I was sick for a couple of days at first. I couldn't get around the house, and didn't have the strength to care for myself. Any time I spoke to anyone I put on my happy face, which would have been a good thing if that was how I really felt. I was embarrassed about my condition. I thought the whole world was laughing at me.

Staying at home was not only a challenge physically, but emotionally. Although there were everyday things I needed to accomplish at home I just couldn't seem to get anything done. Every week after my injection I would feel worse than the week before, I started fainting without cause. What now, I asked myself. Why am I becoming so ill after my injections? A couple of months passed; it was time for my yearly appointment with my cardiologist. Test as usual; Echo cardiogram, which is an ultrasound of the heart. Randy took the afternoon off work so he could take me to the hospital for test. As I lay on the table the technician kept looking at me and then at the screen. After about twenty minutes he excused himself leaving Randy and I in the room alone. He returned and told me my doctor would be contacting me with the results.

The next morning while preparing breakfast the telephone rang, "Eliana this is Dr. Far from cardiology, I received your results from your echo, you are suffering from congestive heart failure, and your ejection fraction is currently twenty-five percent. I need you to stop taking your ms therapy injections, and I have consulted with your neurologist and he will be contacting you shortly."

I sat on the kitchen floor and I could feel the warmth of my tears on my face. Congestive heart failure, I could not express how very tired I was feeling.

Father, Give me strength, Guide me Lord
I love you Lord, I trust you Lord
In Jesus name, Amen.

"Be self-controlled and alert. Your enemy the devil prowls around like a roaring lion looking for someone to devour. Resist him, standing firm in the faith because you know that your brothers throughout the world are undergoing the same kind of sufferings. And the God of all grace, who called you to his eternal glory in Christ, after you have suffered a little while, will himself restore you and make you strong, firm and steadfast. To him be the power for ever and ever. Amen." (1 Peter 5: 8-11)

After a series of test and doctor's appointments it was discovered that the ms therapy injection which I was using carried a two percent risk of causing congestive heart failure in patients with heart conditions. I was in that two percentile. It also appears that three of the four therapies available are made with interferon which seems to be the cause of my problem. There is however one therapy that I can take, which is synthetic, the only drawback about this medication is it must be injected daily. Oh Joy!!!!! I am so not happy about that, but I knew that this is par for my course. The next six months was filled with many ups and downs. I tried to balance everything in my life and felt like I was falling down a very dark hole. During this time period relationships were broken, physical adjustments were necessary, complications occurred, hospitalizations, difficult trials, and great tragedies, but no matter what Randy just seemed to go with it.

Although I was experiencing a very difficult time in my own personal life, I still needed to make time for daddy. His condition was changing and there was significant weight loss. He seemed so happy when the family was together that it was easy to overlook the obvious.

CHAPTER **7**

I Give Up

RANDY JR., RANDY, and I just couldn't see eye to eye on some of our issues, so it became necessary to put time and space between us. That was a very painful time for me because I didn't agree with either one of them, but there was far too much going on in my life to handle any one thing. I understood Randy Jr. Feelings, and I could hear my husband loud and clear. Despite my feelings my stand has and always will be with Randy. I still had a lot to learn about myself and my marriage.

The fall brought great tragedy; Dahlia lost her first born child, a son. She named him Chance'. There were many days of pain and tears to follow. Everyone made themselves available except Randy Jr. and although I couldn't understand the separation between Dahlia and Rand, I did understand his need to stay away. I pray the days ahead bring resolution to this family.

> Heavenly Father, I come before you humbly,
> Hurt and confused, not understanding anything, trusting you Lord
> Thy kingdom come, your will be done,
> On earth as it is in heaven
> Give us the strength to endure, I love you Lord
> Amen.

I began to feel that I spent more time in the hospital than I did at home. Constantly in physical therapy, retraining myself to walk having a constant foot drag, falling and stumbling all the time. Steroid infusions for three to five days, which carried side effects of its own. My church family was always there for me. When Randy had to work, they would alternate and come to my house to help care for me. They would bathe me, help dress me, exercise with me, or just sit with me and pray. After my last steroid infusion I lost the ability to taste anything. That's when I lost my desire for food. I would try to remember what a particular food taste like and imagine tasting it while I was eating it. That didn't work; I could only feel the texture of whatever I put in my mouth. Coffee felt like something warm and gritty, and I never appreciated the very small blessings in life until I was forced to live without them. Losing my sight briefly, brought new meaning to being able to see. Once my taste buds started to return I gained a new appreciation when I prayed for God to bless the food which I was about to receive. Sometimes I needed a cane to get around, and other times I had to use a walker. It was an embarrassment; I was in a battle for my personal independence. I was rejecting my new normal, not realizing this was my new normal I was already living. While I was at church everyone there was very supportive, I counseled with Pastor Austin regularly, he has always been very instrumental in my recovery, with words of encouragement, prayer, or his awesome ability to quietly listen. His presence wasn't only for me, Randy and our children were included. I seemed to have a problem with the way I was viewed by the world, now I was a person with a disability. But it wasn't the world with the problem; it was who I saw in the mirror that was my problem.

These days when I cried, I could no longer tell exactly what I was crying about. Was it because of the baby, Randy Jr., My dad, or my health, which seemed to occupy most of my time? Randy was trying so very hard to console me, but I found myself filled with emotions I could not even explain.

"Trust in the Lord with all your heart, and lean not on your own understanding; In all your ways acknowledge him, and he shall direct your paths. Do not be wise in your own eyes, fear the Lord and depart from evil. It will be health to your flesh, and strength to your bones." (Proverbs 3: 5-8)

One Sunday afternoon after church I decided we should stay home. My body was tired and I felt mentally exhausted. Randy looked at me and asked, "What's for dinner?" I felt a small explosion within my chest, and I no longer had control of myself. Crying uncontrollably I looked at Randy, "We need to separate, divorce, this is too much. Everything is wrong with me and I don't even want you to understand. I am tired of crying, I am tired of hurting, and I am tired of being tired. When you married me I'm sure you didn't intend to sign up for all of this. This is too much for me, so I'm sure this is too much for you." Randy looked at me with tears in his eyes and said, "I say it's time we pray." Angered by his calmness I replied, "You pray, I'm done."

By this time I was crying so hard I couldn't even see. I went into the basement, because it was the lowest point in the house, and I was at the lowest point in my life. I turned off all the lights because I felt surrounded by total darkness anyway. I laid on the floor in the fetal position, having decided that I will stay right here until I cease to exist. As I lay there on the floor in total darkness my head was pounding, my chest hurt and I just kept saying, "No more Lord, no more, I surrender, I can't do this anymore. I'm weak, I'm tired, and plain worn out, are you listening Lord, I'm not moving from this space until I am no more." I couldn't hear anything in the house, just the sound of my own thoughts. "I will not do this any longer!" I just didn't want to feel anything else, I wanted the pain to stop and just disappear into nothingness, and then it happened.

I felt surrounded by quietness, a blessed quietness. I kept hearing, "Peace be still" just say, "Peace be still." No I will not say anything! I will not move until I am no more!!! At that point I was demanding of

God that I cease to exist. "Say it." I could feel the words in my heart. "Just say peace be still and see what happens. No, right now I don't care what happens I will not say anything!! I felt so broken, I believed I had nothing else to give, I could feel my tears creating a puddle on the floor. "Peace be still" I can't I cried, I'm just not strong enough, I don't want to, I'm angry, I'm hurt and I'm tired. I feel so all alone, no one but you Lord truly understand what I am going through: I must be losing my mind. I can't believe that I am having this conversation. This must be a dream. "Peace be still, say it", No, no, no, I muttered, I felt like I was losing my voice. At that moment I realized I was no longer crying. The pain in my heart started to subside. "But I don't want to say Peace be still, I want to exist no more. " The darkness in the basement was overpowering, but the quietness, the stillness of the dark felt surreal. I felt a great sense of calmness. I no longer wanted to fight, so I said it, "Peace be still" I could feel my heart telling me, "Say it again, Peace be still." Each time I said it I felt a sense of peace in my heart until I could hear my own voice, "Peace be still!" I continued to say it, "Peace be still" I soon noticed I was no longer laying on the floor, I was sitting. "Peace be still." I noticed the light shining through the basement windows. What's happening to me, I no longer felt angry. The feeling of hopelessness was gone. "Peace be still." I wasn't afraid anymore; I no longer wanted to disappear, I only want to understand, as I sat there on the floor the tears once again began to flow, I could hear myself saying, "I'm sorry Lord, I lost my focus and I took my eye off you, and started to sink into the darkness. I know this is a storm in my life, and this too shall pass." Wow I was having my own personal pity party. I got up and went upstairs; looking at the clock I could not believe I just spent two and a half hours in the basement. Wow, what just happened I thought to myself, knowing God the way I do how could I just give up on myself like that? My next thought was, sometimes it's much easier to get up when you fall down, than it is to try to stop yourself from falling. What a day this has been for me.

"He got up, rebuked the wind and said to the waves, "Quiet! Be still! Then the wind died down and it was completely calm. (Mark 4: 39)

"Now faith is being sure of what we hope for and certain of what we do not see." (Hebrews 11: 1)

Now is the time to seek some divine order in my life. First I had to confront Randy. An apology was not enough for me, He deserved an explanation. I told him I was sorry for my outburst, my behavior was unexplainable, and unnecessary. I was selfishly feeling sorry for myself, and I only want Randy to be happy, and have a little peace and sunshine. It just seemed like it was one thing after another with me. I was totally overwhelmed and lost my focus. Randy told me everything was okay, he understood, "I love you with all that I am, and all that I am to be, this marriage is ordained." He smiled at me with that twinkle in his eyes, which I fell in love with in the beginning, and I knew he was okay, but for me only one thing could make this right. I took Randy by the hand and said, "Randy, I say it's time we pray." He smiled at me, kissed me gently and helped me get down on my knees, so we could pray together, united as one.

> Lord,
> We come before you, as one body in Christ
> We ask for your forgiveness, we dedicate our lives to you, as well as to each other
> Thank you for peace and understanding, May everything we do glorify you Lord
> May we display unity, always respecting one another
> Maintaining a personal relationship with you, individually and collectively
> And never question our vows
> Thank you Lord, for your grace and mercy
> In Jesus name, Amen.

Having taken the time to rededicate ourselves to one another, I felt good about removing self and allowing God to guide me through. The holidays were right around the bend, and for once I was not looking forward to celebrating, but life does go on. That was a period of time I was always singing, I'll understand it better." The next couple of months I found myself very busy preparing for the holidays. Spending time with daddy, and packing up baby items. Although I managed to keep myself very busy, I also set aside some private time to grieve.

During the holiday season our home was very quiet. I spent as much time as possible with my parents. Daddy didn't talk very much anymore, but we managed to communicate without words. Some days we would just sit side by side and watch TV. Momma had to monitor what daddy watched, because he would interact with whatever was on. He was spending much more time sleeping, and getting him to eat became a full time job for momma. Because I suffered from tremors, as well as leg and arm weakness, I believe his comfort level was a little different with me. There were days when we would sit down to eat and because my hands shook as bad as his we would both sit at the table together and eat with our hands laughing at ourselves. Looking at this man, my daddy, now fragile hurt me, but I was so thankful to God that I still had him. I'll take a little as opposed to none at all.

> "But even if I am being poured out like a drink offering on the sacrifice and service coming from your faith, I am glad and rejoice with all of you. So you too should be glad and rejoice with me." (Philippians 2: 17-18)

CHAPTER 8

Dreaded Phone Calls

I FOUND MYSELF getting back into a groove, a way of doing things that worked for me, and then the telephone rang. It was momma, "Eliana, I want you to sit down." I instantly thought it was daddy. "What is it momma, is daddy okay? Daddy is fine baby, its Jacob, I don't know what happened but Jacob is dead." I heard her, but I didn't understand what she was saying. Jacob is my sister Tamera's son, my first thought was Jacob was hit by a car. Momma continued to speak. "He's at the hospital, Tamera and Art are there." I was numb, no tears just confusion. Then the phone rang again, it was Raina, she was hysterical. I told her I would be there in a minute. I drove to Riana's house totally bewildered. By the time I got to Raina, Malcolm was there standing in her kitchen. Raina was crying saying she didn't understand what was happening. Malcolm explained to us we need to pull ourselves together and remain calm for Tamera's sake. We drove to the hospital in silence. I later learned Jacob got up that morning, same as he did every morning, and Tamera helped him get ready for school as she did every day. The school bus pulled up and Jacob ran off to meet the bus, but today before he stepped on the bus he turned to his mom and waved goodbye. After school he returned home from school, asked for his favorite meal; then told his dad he wanted to take a bath. Jacob got into the tub and died shortly after. We must always cherish every moment as if it is our last, because one day it will be.

I was concerned about daddy, how he would take losing a grandchild. If attending a funeral would cause him too much grief. If it would cause depression and daddy would give up. After hearing everyone's input momma made the decision daddy would attend. I prayed for strength for my family, and tried to support Tamera any way I could. The next five days were tough, the entire family was in turmoil, through all my heartache I was okay, I had already reached my deepest depth of darkness and God brought me back. I felt there was nowhere to go but up.

Randy seemed withdrawn, I noticed but didn't pay it much attention. So much has been going on with me I assumed Randy was grieving as well. Regardless to any situation we always took time out to pray together.

Once again things seem to get back to normal, well my new normal which was nothing like life use to be for me. Momma resumed taking daddy to adult day care, it was a good way for daddy to have some activities, and momma to have some time to herself, after all taking care of daddy was not easy and she too was up in age. Daddy was doing as well as expected. His weight was down, but his spirit was good. I think he reached a level of acceptance, meaning he understood what was going on with his body. We continued to visit as often as possible. Communication became difficult with daddy, every time someone asked daddy a question momma responded, and that really bothered me. I started asking momma to please let daddy answer when I ask him a question. Her response was he can't answer you, but I only wanted her to let him try. I felt she was being overbearing and that was the cause of his silence. I just wanted to hear his voice, to hear him say anything even if it didn't make any sense. I would have to catch myself, the tone I would use with momma, I had to remind myself, that's her husband, but that's also my daddy. Being a wife and a mother I should know better, but my feelings were certainly getting the best of me. Daddy continued to talk about going home, but not as much as he used to. I was glad about that; my heart was full right now. It's time to just take one day at a time, "Do all that you need to do today." Daddy's words echo in my memory, and so I shall daddy, so I shall.

> "Honor your father and you mother, that your days may be long upon the land which the Lord your God is giving you." (Exodus 20: 12)

> "Honor your father and mother, which is the first commandment with promise. That it may go well with you and that you may enjoy long life on the earth. Fathers, do not exasperate your children; instead, bring them up in the training and instruction of the Lord." (Ephesians 6: 2-4)

Randy was turning fifty this year, and we needed to do something special. He seemed to be under so much pressure at work, and at home. Then I decided a birthday party for Randy would be wonderful. It was about time to bring some positivity into the house. Food, fun, and fellowship is the way to go. I devised a guest list and a menu, I asked my family for help, and the planning began.

Randy resumed his skating every Friday, and although we did everything together he was adamant about going skating on Fridays with or without me. This was totally unusual behavior for Randy when it came to me. I didn't understand, but so much has been going on that I felt this was a battle better left unfought.

Daddy was sleeping a lot lately, all the time it seemed; he wasn't eating very much and would hold on to the same glass of water all day. It didn't matter what anyone said he was going to have his way. Two stubborn men in my life at the same time, are you kiddin me? I was going to have to find a happy medium in dealing with them both. As the seasons changed so did daddy's condition. After visiting one Sunday I called my sister Jaclyn to talk with her.

"Daddy isn't doing very well" I said, "I can just look at him and tell. I noticed that too" Jaclyn replied. "He's sleeping all the time, he isn't eating and has lost a considerable amount of weight, and I don't think he has much time left." Although Jaclyn's tone was calm her words pierced my heart. I could feel my heart breaking because I knew she was right. It was in his eyes. The fight was gone, when he smiled I could see a sense of peace, I could tell he was happy. I continued to plan Randy's birthday party knowing there was so much I needed to do. Some days I was so excited I would ask God, "Lord, I just want to celebrate Randy's birthday and not deal with a tragedy, not at the same time." Realizing how very selfish that was I started to pray.

> Father, Forgive my selfishness
> Your will, will be done
> Mold my heart; I need to stay on your agenda
> Strengthen me
> May all I do bring glory to your name
> Amen.

Randy's party was rapidly approaching and I was so busy between planning and visiting daddy I didn't bother to take notice to much else. When Randy wasn't at work he was helping me around the house. The yard was our favorite pass time, but Randy started to complain about it. He would go to work and leave his keys at home or his ID badge. He seemed to fuss a lot lately, and I didn't understand why, and I began not to care. I figured Randy got out of the house once a week, get it out of your system at the skating rink, and leave it there. We still took time to pray together, but something was different, I couldn't put my finger on it so I guess it can't be that important. Wrong again.

The end of summer quickly approached and it was time for Randy's party. I called Randy Jr. and told him about it, but after a no show for Dahlia after she lost the baby, and a no show for Jacob's funeral, I really didn't expect an appearance. By this time I was okay about everything going on. God will give us all that he wants us to have, and all that we don't have we either aren't ready for or we don't need it. That was my only way of keeping peace in my heart. Randy's party went on without a hitch. It was wonderful. Everyone was in attendance except Randy Jr. I really wanted him to be there, but knowing how much like Randy he is I knew he would be a no show. At that point my anger turned into pain. Something is going to have to give when it comes to these two men, but what? Only God can guide me through this mess that we created. God being the awesome God he is does everything in his time and so I shall wait. I shook my feelings, put on my happy face and resumed my duties as hostess. There were speeches and tears, laughter and food. My parents did not attend, but their day being uneventful was the best gift ever. Randy had a wonderful time and making him happy was my ultimate goal.

Randy and I were still driving the church van on first Sundays. I found joy in spending time with Randy and the mothers of our church, but I started to notice Randy needed me to navigate him to every ones house. This is strange I thought, he has spent most of his career on the roads of this city, how could he not know the streets. Every month it took longer to pick up and drop every one off. Maybe he is so overwhelmed by everything going on with me and my family. He's just preoccupied and that's understandable.

One Sunday afternoon while sitting in my parent's backyard, my sister and I started a discussion on all the things around the house that needed to be done. "Momma can't keep up the house and take care of daddy." Jaclyn said; we each need to pick a room and spend the day thoroughly cleaning. We each agreed on which chores we would take, picked a day of the week and agreed to do it while daddy was at day care.

The day came and we met at my parent's house early. We kissed daddy goodbye turned the music up, and started cleaning. There was so much to do I didn't think one day would be enough. Jaclyn took the living and dining room, Cadence took the kitchen, and I was elected to clean the bathroom. Raina was suppose to vacuum and mop, Tamera still grieving from the loss of Jacob decided to go to work, but she sent carpet cleaners in her absence.

When we finished cleaning we were all very pleased with what we accomplished. Later that evening Jaclyn and I talked on the phone. "Eliana is it just me or did it feel like we were cleaning the house in preparation for a funeral? I know it felt really strange at the house today. I didn't want to say anything because I didn't want to upset anyone." Everyone was so sensitive when it came to daddy. If Jaclyn hadn't brought it up I would have never said anything about my feelings at all. I felt a sense of dread; I could tell something was coming. Daddy has been battling Alzheimer's disease for the last eight years. Now he's sleeping a lot, not eating well, and his weight was down considerably. The thought of being without daddy was over whelming, and I had to stop everything I was doing for a couple of minutes and cry.

> Lord, I know I am being prepared
> Bless me with knowledge, and wisdom
> Bless our home; I need to be encouraging, glorifying you
> I ask for a song in my heart
> Thank you Lord, for being God
> I love you, Amen.

The end of summer was fast approaching. I was trying to mentally prepare for the change of seasons, because that meant a change for daddy. His birthday was coming up in a couple of weeks and we needed to discuss what we were going to do for his birthday. I was deep in my thoughts when I was interrupted by what else, the telephone, it was Raina, "Eliana, we are taking daddy to the hospital; it appears he laid down for a nap and we can't wake him. He hasn't been drinking enough water and Tamera believes he is dehydrated." Oh boy I thought here we go. I called Randy at work with the news, and we agreed to go to the hospital as soon as he arrived home.

"A word was secretly brought to me, my ears caught a whisper of it. Amid disquieting dreams in the night, when deep sleep falls on men," (Job 4: 12-13)

The doctor's said daddy was in a coma like sleep due to dehydration. All of his vital signs were okay, so they gave him IV fluids and told us all we could do was wait. I knew that was going to be the hard part. So we waited, and waited by his bedside praying that daddy would wake up soon.

Sunday morning was beautiful, sunny and warm. Randy and I got up showered and was getting ready for church when Tamera called, "Daddy's awake" I could feel the tears starting to flow. "Thank you Jesus" I whispered, "Randy there seems to be a change of plans, instead of going to church were going to the hospital, daddy is awake!" I was so excited about seeing daddy awake. Tamera said he was eating and drinking and talking. We drove all the way to the hospital with me singing and dancing in my seat. As we were walking up to the hospital doors Tamera was sitting on the bench outside of the door crying. "Tamera what's wrong? Its daddy, he's talking, but the thing he's saying bothers me. He wants to talk with each of us." Then she said, "Daddy is in the end stage of Alzheimer's." I sat down on the bench beside her and placed my hand on hers. I know this hard for you because of all the things you are dealing with, but we're going to be okay. I can only imagine how you feel." At that moment I wondered, am I speaking about Jacob or daddy. I knew I needed to walk away. I didn't want to make her feel any worse. "I'm going to go up to daddy's room now I'll see you up there shortly." Once I reached daddy's floor, I noticed Shamar walking towards the elevators, and the air seemed heavy. As Shamar walked by he said, "I don't even want to deal with this."

Deal with what? If daddy is awake and talking, what's the problem? I thought to myself. Some of my siblings along with their children were sitting in the waiting area; I spoke to everyone and kept walking. Randy decided he would wait in the waiting area and give me a moment with daddy. Wow, I thought that's different, Randy has always been by my side, but my focus was on getting to the room. When I reached the room daddy was sitting up in the bed, momma was sitting by his bedside, and Sabrina, Malcolm, and Wade were present. "Hi daddy," I said with a smile, "Eliana he replied, sit down." Sabrina and Malcolm were busy trying to get daddy to eat but it appeared he didn't want anything else to eat. All he seems to want to do is talk. Daddy had something he wanted to share with each of his children. Without knowing what happened before I arrived, I assumed he already spoke with the children that were upset. But he's awake what could he possibly say that would upset someone. Jaclyn walked into the room shortly after I did, and daddy seemed so very happy to see her. He called her Jac for short. Then he started to speak.

"Malcolm I want you to give Jaclyn twenty-five dollars." I was amused by this and started to laugh. "Okay daddy I will." Malcolm replied. "Eliana" he called, I walked close to his side, "Yes daddy, take good care of yourself. I will daddy, I replied, "And look after Jaclyn." At that point I'm sure my facial expression changed as well as my tone. "Look after Jaclyn, are you kiddin me? Look after Jaclyn!" I started to laugh uncontrollably, "Jaclyn only had a stroke daddy, and I have Multiple sclerosis, who the heck is going to take care of me?" At this point everyone in the room was laughing, while I continued to fuss, "You tell me to take care of myself, and then turn around and tell me to take care of Jaclyn." Daddy's facial expression never changed, he was pleasant but serious. Jaclyn just laughed pointing at me, "Daddy told you to take care of me Ha!" I stuck out my tongue at her, "Are you feeling special, well I think not!" Then daddy touched my hand looked at me and said, "Eliana, I will always be with you," I began to feel a tug at my heart, and my eyes started to water. I felt a need to show him that I was strong and could handle this, so I closed my eyes for a second, help me Lord, give me strength. I opened my eyes and replied, "I know that daddy." He looked at me making sure we made eye contact, "But you won't be able to see me." It took every ounce of everything God gave me not to fall into his arms and cry like a baby. Looking back I really wished I had, because I was his baby, but instead I replied unable to hold back my tears any longer, "That's okay daddy I don't have to see you, because you live in my heart, you will always be a part of my heart." I kissed daddy on his forehead, and at that point I needed to leave the room. I now understood why everyone was in such a somber mood. Daddy continued to speak with each of us as we waited for the doctors to come in. When the doctor finally arrived, they said daddy was well enough to go home, the IV fluids rehydrated him, and we just need to make sure he drinks enough fluids daily. I believe daddy just spent the last two days talking with God. He now has an understanding which we will never understand.

> Our Father, Which art in heaven, hallowed be thy name, Thy kingdom come, Thy will be done,
> In earth, as it is in heaven, Give us this day our daily bread, and forgive us our trespass
> As we forgive those who trespass against us, and lead us not into temptation,
> But deliver us from evil, for thine is the Kingdom, and the power
> And the glory, forever
> Amen.

We all accompanied momma and daddy home excited about him being awake. As soon as daddy walked up the driveway he started pointing out things that he wanted done. "This grass along the fence needs to be removed." He was speaking as though someone was taking notes. Daddy walked into the house and spent the next thirty minutes telling us all the things he wanted done inside the house. When he was finished he decided he wanted to go for a walk. I stood at the end of the driveway and watched daddy and Malcolm walk to the end of the street. I wished I knew what instructions he was giving Malcolm.

We all sat at the dining room table to discuss our new plan of action. "Momma needs someone here to help take care of daddy." I was relieved Jaclyn spoke first. "Daddy needs much more attention now. I will come over on Mondays and stay thru the week. I'll go home on Fridays, that way momma and daddy aren't here alone anymore, sometimes you stand a greater risk of losing the caregiver before the person being cared for dies." Tamera confirmed that daddy needs help around the clock, along with a health care nurse in the house, because his condition is progressing. "Daddy is now in the end stage of Alzheimer's and doesn't have much time left. We need to see to it that he receives the best care possible." I spoke in agreement with Tamera and Jaclyn, and that's when the arguments began. Cadence felt Jaclyn was not in authority to spend time at the house, because she didn't spend enough time with the family. As a whole, Raina was upset because it sounds like we were giving daddy permission to die. Malcolm announced that if anything happened to daddy he would be of no use to anyone. Shamar got up from the table and left. At that point I felt it was my turn to express myself, everyone was already hyped, so I had nothing to lose. "I agree with Jaclyn, this is the cycle of life, and daddy doesn't need our permission to die, but when he is ready, not only will I tell him it's okay, but I will be okay with it." That comment really seemed to set Cadence off. "Well I'll never give daddy permission to die, never!!" Tamera began to cry, is this because of Jacob or daddy I thought to myself. Cadence pushed away from the table and went outside.

Although our round table discussion was finished. I believed we all had an understanding.

Because I was available during the day I told Jaclyn I would come to the house in the morning and Randy would pick me up after he got off of work. Everything seemed to be going well; the nurse was scheduled to come out on Friday. Jaclyn stayed at the house, and I came by during the day, daddy was happy and momma could get some rest.

Friday came and the nurse arrived. After daddy's intake examination; the nurse explained daddy met the criteria for hospice. In other words, it was time for daddy to start his hospice care. Tamera spoke honestly with Jaclyn and me prior to this happening, so we were not surprised, however everyone else was quite upset with this decision. The nurse explained they were sending out a hospice nurse to fill out all the additional paperwork, and it was time for momma to make a decision about signing a DNR order, DNR meaning do not recessitate. Raina and Cadence were strongly against that, but momma said that's what daddy wanted. Daddy sat in silence; he had nothing to say about anything. She told us the hospice nurse will have the DNR paperwork, momma signed the papers and daddy's hospice care began. Jaclyn decided since daddy is in hospice, she would just stay there until she didn't need to. Although some didn't seem happy about that, I was very thankful to Jaclyn for doing something selfless like this; how can people justify being upset over something they aren't even willing to do themselves. Randy and I drove home in silence and for the first time I asked Randy to go skating so I could be alone for just a little while. No tears, I just needed some quiet time with God.

"Be still, and know that I am God. I will be exalted among the nations, I will be exalted in the earth!" (Psalms 46: 10)

CHAPTER 9

What Is Hospice?

HOSPICE IS A special concept of care designed to provide comfort and support to patients and their families when a life-limiting illness no longer responds to cure-oriented treatments. The goal of Hospice care is to improve the quality of patients last days by offering comfort and dignity.

The next morning I woke refreshed and ready for whatever the day had in store for me. We decided to barbeque. Sunday dinner on a warm September Saturday afternoon sounds like a plan, I thought to myself. Randy and I dressed and went to my parent's house.

Daddy was in such a good mood. He was playful, happy, and walking around talking with everyone. It felt just like a holiday, everyone being present at the same time. Daddy didn't eat much, but he behaved like a man on a mission. After dinner Cadence cleaned the kitchen, and one by one everyone left the house. Before I knew it there was only Tamera, Jaclyn, Randy and I left. Randy was sitting in the den watching television, I was standing in the kitchen, and momma was getting ready for bed. Daddy was standing in the bedroom by the door when he called for Tamera to come in. Jaclyn got up as well to see if she could help with something. When Tamera walked into the room daddy looked at her and said, "Tamera I want you to get a really nice suit to wear, and I don't want a long service, short and sweet. I'm not trying to hear that daddy, but okay." Tamera responded,

Jaclyn walked into the kitchen our eyes locked, "Did you hear that Eliana? She said, "Yea I heard that, he's talking to Tamera about his funeral arrangements." Jaclyn turned and walked away and I resumed playing with daddy's hat on the kitchen counter.

Tamera decided it was time for her to go home and Daddy walked her to the door. They were laughing and playing. Tamera always played with daddy trying to touch his neck, because his neck was so sensitive. I told Randy I was ready to go, and I walked to the door so we could leave out when Tamera did. As I passed by daddy, he grabbed my shirt collar and pulled me close to him saying, "You better not leave!" I looked into his eyes grabbed his collar and said, "I'm not going anywhere!" I wasn't sure what just happened, was God speaking to me through daddy? Or did daddy just want me to stay? At this point it didn't matter. I took Randy into the living room and explained to him what just happened. "This is your path Eliana; you only get one chance to do the right thing. Only do what you know you can live with, because you're going to have to. There are no do-over's when it comes to life and death. Stay because your dad needs you to, or stay because he asked you, or stay because you can. I'll come by everyday to see you after work; everything is going to be okay." I stood there in amazement, Randy and I have never spent one night apart since we married, but I knew he was right. So I told Randy to take me home so I could pack my clothes, because I'm staying here with momma and daddy.

Monday morning there was a knock at the door; it was April (daddy's hospice nurse). After she introduced herself to the family she assessed daddy. She then sat down with momma, Jaclyn, Cadence, Raina, and I. She proceeded to explain the importance of family counseling both group and individual therapy. Then she explained her reasons why. "Death brings out the worst in people, and even the best and closest families have a difficult time during this process." Raina assured her, "We are far different than most families, we don't fight, we discuss everything together; I'm sure we won't have any problems when it comes to that. Now comes the difficult part."

April took the DNR papers from the folder, Raina and Cadence were visibly disturbed, but Jaclyn and I had already talked with momma about this. Cadence and Raina tried to talk momma out of signing the DNR, but Jaclyn and I assured her that if that was what she wanted we would back her by any means necessary. Despite the glares from my sisters, momma signed the DNR, and for now April's work was done. April left her contact numbers and told us she would be coming by once a week unless we call her or something happens.

> "Consider what God has done; who can straighten what he has made crooked? When times are good, be happy; but when times are bad, consider: God has made the one as well as the other. Therefore, a man cannot discover anything about his future." (Ecclesiastes 7: 13-14)

Jaclyn and I worked well together, and we didn't fall short on fun and games. Daddy seemed to enjoy the laughter, and practal jokes we often played on each other. He needed assistance with everything. We watched him closely because we had a fear of him falling. I called Pastor Austin, and informed him of everything going on. He came by the house the following day to meet with momma and daddy.

After greeting everyone Pastor Austin sat down on the couch beside daddy, and read some scriptures to him. Daddy never said a word, but tears started to flow from his eyes. I could tell he understood everything Pastor Austin was saying. When he finished he turned his attention to momma. "I don't know where you stand as far as a church home goes, but I would like to take you and your husband in as members of our church. Randy and Eliana are long time members in good standing with the church and as a member you can receive the same benefits as any other member." Momma thanked Pastor Austin and asked to become members of our church family.

I sat there in my chair overwhelmed by the compassion Pastor Austin showed me and my family. I thanked him for his presence and walked him to the door. "And how are you doing Eliana?" Pastor Austin was very good at reading my expressions. "I'm okay" I said without hesitation. The way he was looking at me I could tell he was reading my emotions. "I will come by at least once a week to visit with your dad, but I want to meet with you as well once a week. Maybe you and Randy can meet with me at your house so we can talk one on one. I need to know how you are handling this or if you are handling this at all. I thanked Pastor Austin for everything, set a day to meet with him, and resumed my day.

Being there in the house with momma and daddy everyday was very interesting. Daddy didn't talk a lot at first, but as time passed we noticed he had quite a bit to say. What I didn't realize is I would soon grow tired of everyone else talking.

Daddy was sitting on the couch watching TV and I noticed he was scratching his head a lot. "Do you need your hair washed Daddy?" Daddy looked at me and shook his head yes. "Come with me and have a seat." I sat daddy in a chair outside of the bathroom, and wrapped a towel around his shoulders. Using a wash cloth I wet his hair. I washed his hair for him; this was my labor of love. Although I was doing this for daddy it was actually for me. I gained so much from this experience. God is giving me a chance to give back something daddy always gave to me; unconditional love. He sat in that chair trying his best to stay awake while I massaged and combed his hair. What an intimate moment, no words just daddy and me sharing a moment in time. After I dried his hair and told him I was finished, he went into his pocket pulled out his wallet and tried to give Jaclyn five dollars. We later laughed about that. Daddy was a barber by trade, and the rule was, when you get out of the chair you've got to pay the barber. That was the first of many private moments with daddy.

> "Dear friends, let us love one another, for love comes from God. Everyone who loves has been born of God and knows God. " (1 John 4: 7)

Jaclyn and I spent the next five days getting adjusted to our surroundings and sharing our space. Although Tamera went to work every day, she kept very close tabs on what was going on with daddy. She showed us how to properly care for daddy, and when she was there she made sure we were aware of everything regarding his condition. Randy came by every day after work, and we would spend time talking or going for walks. He always knew what to say to me although his presence was encouraging enough. Dahlia came by at least four days a week, making sure we had enough fresh coffee to drink, because the coffee had become our new best friend. Raina came by every day, and had lunch with momma and daddy. That always gave us a chance for rest. Malcolm, Cadence, Wade, and Shamar were there every day after work. Shamar explained to us that he could not help with daddy, but if Jaclyn and I needed anything, he would do his best to provide it for us. Malcolm made sure anything we said daddy need he provided. Cadence and Wade wasn't sure what to do, so they were there to help with whatever. Jaclyn and I gave everyone a full report daily on Daddy's activities, how he felt; what he did, as well as anything he said. I usually did the cooking, while Jaclyn did most of the cleaning. When it came to daddy's grooming momma took care of that.

By the time we entered the second week of hospice everyone had found their groove, but I was growing physically tired. I was beginning to experience muscle spasms in my back, and nerve pain in my legs from assisting with daddy. I prayed to God that I would not have a MS relapse, because that would take me away from whatever daddy needed. God doesn't give you a task without the tools necessary to complete that task. So I trusted God would give me the strength to endure knowing everything would work to God's glory. Jaclyn and I didn't sleep much, we found ourselves up at night talking or reading to daddy, caring for his needs or just watching him sleep. Although everyone was there every day after work Jaclyn or I would be called on to tend to any chores. Everyone was gone by eight o' clock, and every day was the same thing; Raina came in for lunch, Malcolm,

Cadence, Wade and Shamar were there after work, and everyday everyone had questions. Tamera still grieving was as helpful and supportive as she could be, having classes to go to after work, she came whenever she had free time, and in her free time she would prepare meals, or do anything to give Jaclyn and I a break. Most of daddy's children although not very helpful with physical labor, were at least supportive. I didn't mind the questions much, but Raina started coming into the house giving orders, and that was a problem for me.

> Lord, give me strength to endure
> Guide my tongue, so that I am not offensive to anyone
> Guide my feet, so I don't step on anyone's feeling
> Touch my heart, so I may show compassion to all those I encounter
> Thank you Lord, for your unfailing love
> Amen.

After an all night discussion, and reading of scriptures Jaclyn and I decided to do our best to care for daddy despite how anyone made us feel.

Before I knew it the weekend was here, and what would a sunny Saturday afternoon be without a barbeque. Malcolm picked up some meat and started the grill; Tamera was in the kitchen preparing all the side dishes. She told Jaclyn and me to relax, so I went into the living room to take a nap and Jaclyn went into the den to watch TV. We didn't get much sleep the night before because daddy didn't have a good night. He was awake most of the night restless. Although I could hear every one talking, my need for sleep was stronger and I dosed off thanking God for a moment of peace. Daddy sat in the kitchen watching everything going on. My sister Sabrina and her husband Mike arrived later in the afternoon. The day seemed to be going quite well and everyone was having a good time, then I heard Jaclyn. "Sabrina what in the world are you doing?" Her voice was raised. I covered my face with the pillow, but left enough space so I could hear. "I'm taking daddy outside, it's so nice out I asked him if he wanted to go and he said yes" Sabrina replied. "Well you can't just take him to the stairs and let him walk out by himself" said Jaclyn, "You have to have someone walk down the stairs in front of him, and hold him so he doesn't fall" now Jaclyn sounded agitated. I got up and as I entered the kitchen Sabrina was already at the side door, she turned around and came back. "I handle patients all day long, I know what I'm doing, and I don't need you to tell me how to handle him." I looked out of the kitchen window and saw daddy walking pass by himself. "Oh my God," I said. Jaclyn's agitation turned to anger, "You can't just let daddy walk off by himself. What if he fell on the concrete, what if he just wondered off?" By this time Sabrina was quite angry as well. "We are all outside and every one will look after daddy he's fine.

"Why couldn't she just ask someone to help her, what makes me so angry is she does this for a living, and I know she wouldn't let one of her Alzheimer's patients in hospice walk down stairs or anywhere else without the proper assistance, so why do it with daddy." We heard the side door close, and by the time we reached the kitchen daddy was standing there alone. Jaclyn and I stood there looking at one another in amazement. There was no one else there. Daddy came into the house and up the stairs by himself. I could feel the heat of my breath on my lips, and my eyes started to water. I felt angry enough to fight. Is Sabrina in a total state of denial, or is it that Sabrina doesn't believe that daddy is sick, what in the world is she thinking? I needed to walk away, daddy was okay, back in the house safely and Jaclyn sat in the kitchen with him. I went back into the living room to lie down, but too upset to rest. Sleep deprivation, physical pain, and grief are always a bad combination. I was dealing with them all. I thought to myself, this cannot end well.

> "The end of a matter is better than its beginning, and patience is better than pride. Do not be quickly provoked in your spirit, for anger resides in the lap of fools." (Ecclesiastes 7: 8-9)

Outside Sabrina began to explain to Raina and Cadence what happened, and how Jaclyn made her feel. That seemed to irritate Raina, and I can only assume that was her reason for coming into the house. As I lay on the couch in the living room begging myself to go to sleep Jaclyn enters. "I don't understand their problem: I'm in the kitchen and in walk Raina and Cadence packing attitudes like weapons. They're telling me I am behaving like a mother hen, and I am out of order. Cadence said I have no right telling Sabrina what to do with daddy. I sat up on the couch, "What did you say" I asked her. "I told them both if Sabrina knew what she was doing , and not stuck on stupid when it comes to daddy we wouldn't be having this conversation." I paused for a moment, "You know what, I'm getting ready to do right now," I said reaching for my bible. "I'm going to read my scriptures, pray for peace and take a nap. This is only a problem, because we have too many chiefs and two Indians. Jaclyn suggested I read the book of Matthew, and walked into another room. I then opened by bible and started to read.

> "Do not suppose that I have come to bring peace to the earth. I did not come to bring peace, but a sword. For I have come to turn a man against his father, a daughter against her mother, a daughter-in-law against her mother-in-law; a man's enemies will be the members of his own household. Anyone who loves his father or mother more than me is not worthy of me, anyone who loves his son or daughter more than me is not worthy of me, and anyone who does not take his cross and follow me is not worthy of me. Whoever finds his life will lose it, and whoever loses his life for my sake will find it. (Matthew 10: 34-39)

The rest of the day was quite odd, no more outburst, but all of daddy's girls were dressed in camouflage. Pretending we are happy, pretending that we're getting along, and doing it with smiles on our faces. All I knew is if I could just make it to seven o' clock without saying a word, everyone would be gone anyway.

It was eight o' clock and the last person finally left. We locked up the house for the night, and prepared for bed. For the first time since childhood I was not looking forward to Sunday dinner with the family. I miss Randy so much, his presence is so comforting, but I could hear his voice in my mind, "Eliana I say it's time to pray."

Father,
I am angry with my family; I ask that you give me wisdom, and knowledge
So that everything I do, and everything I say glorifies you
Forgive me for my trespasses, keep me focused
May my actions bring my family closer to you
I don't want to behave in a way that my family thinks I'm playing Christian
Keep me strong in my faith, and close to your word
I love you Lord, In Jesus name
Amen.

Although we all retired for the night I could hear daddy's voice. Who is he talking to I thought to myself? So I got up and went into their bedroom doorway. Momma was asleep, but daddy was laying there talking. "Who are you talking to daddy, I asked. John he replied." I stood there puzzled then I asked, "Uncle John daddy? Yes" he said. He's right there, he said pointing across the room. I don't know why but I looked across the room to the nothing that I knew was there. Uncle John; daddy's brother passed away sixteen years ago. "Okay daddy, goodnight," I whispered. I lay on the couch and I could feel a tear rolling down to the pillow. "Lord, I whispered, daddy is having a conversation with his dead brother, I don't understand the close of one's life, and I'm sure in his mind he can see Uncle John, but I have no desire to witness anybody's presence." I chuckled to myself. "Goodnight Eliana" I said aloud, and closed my eyes praying for a better day tomorrow.

"Let me understand the teaching of your precepts, then I will meditate on your wonders. My soul is weary with sorrow; strengthen me according to you word." (Psalm 119: 27-28)

CHAPTER 10

Divided We Will Fall

I AWOKE THE next morning feeling refreshed and renewed. After I showered and dressed, I was ready for whatever this new day had in store for me. The telephone rang, it was Sabrina. She told momma she and Mike were on their way over. When momma hung up the phone she was upset. "What's wrong momma, why are you so angry? That was Sabrina on the phone, and she asked me if I could cook Mike breakfast when they arrive." I stood there biting my lip thinking to myself, here we go again. "Well did you tell her no" I asked. "Eliana I just said okay." I decided today was not going to be a repeat of yesterday. "Well that's just unacceptable." I reached for the phone and dialed Sabrina's number. When she answered I could detect the attitude in her voice. "Good morning Sabrina, Good morning, she replied very dry. You guys haven't eaten breakfast yet, and I'm sure you are going to drive past fifty McDonalds before you get here, why don't you stop and grab something to eat on your way so momma doesn't have to cook." Based on Sabrina's tone I could tell she was livid. " Who do you think you are telling me to pick something up to eat, first of all Mike doesn't eat McDonalds, second I ask momma if she could make Mike something to eat, and she said yes, so if she doesn't have a problem why do you? Sabrina, the only reason I called you back is because Jaclyn and I are here to help momma take care of daddy; why would you give her something else to do! I will deal with this when I get there; she said and hung up the phone. Although I probably shouldn't have said anything to Sabrina I felt being there to help defeated the purpose if someone was bringing more work into the house.

Before Sabrina arrived Raina came into the house. "I've decided to come over early instead of going to church." But the tone in her voice told me she already talked to Sabrina, and was there to pick up where Sabrina left off. I was sitting in the dining room at the table when Raina walked in. She slammed her belongings down on the table, looked at me, turned and walked away. I am far too old for this, I thought to myself. I got up from the table prepared to confront my sister, tell her how I felt, where she could go, and how to get there. She was not the only angry bird in this house. Then I was reminded of my prayer "Keep me focused. May my actions bring my family closer to you?" Well I knew at that point if I opened my mouth that would go right out the window, so I cancelled my plans for confrontation, went into the living room opened my bible, and started to read. There is no way my family would see the love of God through my poor behavior and messed up attitude, and there was no way I could adjust my attitude without the love of God.

I tried very hard to maintain silence throughout the day, only doing what daddy or momma needed. But watching my sisters huddle up, whisper back and forth, laugh and joke until I entered the room and then fall silent or leave the room was really starting to annoy me. Watching this unfold, I was reminded of the days which I was a part of that, behaving the same way with my sisters just because someone didn't agree. "Thank you for showing me this Lord is this what I looked like. I used to behave just like that. Thank you for growth and change." I asked God to help me; give me strength to withstand. I do understand everyone is grieving, and hurt people usually hurt people. I only ask that my physical pain subside, and my emotional pain decrease.

Daddy was sitting in the kitchen at the table when I entered the room. Raina was trying to get him to drink some juice. Daddy pushed the glass away, but Raina was persistent. This time I spoke knowing there would be words, but there were things I wanted to say and this was the perfect opportunity. I picked up the glass and moved it to the counter. Raina looked at me with her eyes piercing mine. "Eliana let's step outside, I want to talk to you!" We stood in the driveway beside her vehicle. "You need to understand one thing, she said speaking to me as if I were one of her children. Daddy has ten children, and if each of us wants to give him a glass of juice we can! You have no right, nor is it your place to tell me or anyone else what they can or cannot do when it comes to daddy. We all love him and want to take care of him, and you are totally out of order taking charge like some mother hen, nobody has left you in charge!" The entire time she was fussing, I stood there taking it all in quietly, allowing her to get all of her feelings out. "Are you finished, I asked? Yes daddy does have ten children, but only two are here twenty-four seven, I know everyone wants to help, but help where It's needed, not where you choose. Maybe he's been drinking juice all day, but you wouldn't know that, because you weren't here. Maybe I am like a mother hen; tell me Raina, what does a mother hen do? Raina opened her mouth to speak, and I just cut her off. "I let you speak with no interruptions now it's my turn." I continued in a calm even tone. "Sabrina told you what I said to her, but she neglected to tell you why. First thing this morning she called the house and told your mother to cook breakfast for her husband. Mike is Sabrina's responsibility not mommas. The reason we are all here is to help momma take care of daddy, because it has become too much for her to do alone. So Sabrina needs to check her foolishness at the door, and try to be a help instead of a hindrance. I don't have an issue with sharing anything that needs to be done around here, but I'm tired of listening to you tell me what I should be doing, and then you turn around and go home, sleep in the comfort of your own bed with your husband. I volunteered for this sacrifice, and glad to do it, but I am not a part of the hired help. I too am one of daddy's children, and being here around the clock with daddy I have a pretty good idea of what he needs. So, I suggest what you need to do at this point is either step up or shut up, meaning stop talking about it and be about it!" Raina just stood there looking at me livid. Her voice was raised. I just don't appreciate the way you act when we get here. You go off by yourself, and you don't really talk to anybody. I'm here every day, and I always do what I can." At that moment I realized Raina was more hurt than angry. "Raina I don't want you to be mad, I just want you to understand I'm tired, I'm hurting, and I'm in physical pain. Anything you do for daddy when you are here I appreciate, but while you are here I need to rest. I'm not trying to step on anybody's toes, just back up off of me, and know that I am doing the best that I can with what I have. Besides it wouldn't hurt any of you guys to spend the night, or even a weekend here." Raina nodded, turned and walked into the backyard to talk with Sabrina. I went into the kitchen to sit with daddy.

As I walked into the house it appeared I walked into the end of a heated discussion between Jaclyn and Cadence. After having a heated discussion of my own I was not interested in what was said. So I quietly stood beside daddy. Raina came in and sat down beside Cadence. Jaclyn and I stood by the doorway. The room was silent and the air will filled with disharmony. I the mist of the silence daddy spoke; "You girls be nice to one another" he spoke with a stern tone. "Did you hear that" Raina said standing up, "Daddy said be nice to me" I laughed and looked at Jaclyn. Let it go I thought to myself. Raina walked over and touched daddy shoulder, "What is it daddy" Raina leaned over, "Be safe and be smart." Raina looked a little puzzled. "What do you mean daddy" she asked, "That's all I have to say" Daddy hunched his shoulders, and resumed looking out of the kitchen window. At this point I just wanted this day to be over with. I was glad when they started putting the lawn chairs away, but before leaving the house Sabrina, Cadence, and Raina made sure I knew they decided to spend the night on Thursday. Oh Lord, my strength, and my redeemer, help me. I was truly looking forward to my weekly counseling session with Pastor Austin.

"A man's steps are directed by the Lord. How then can anyone understand his own way" (Proverbs 20: 24)

"A man of knowledge uses words with restraint, and a man of understanding is even-tempered. Even a fool is thought wise if he keeps silent, and discerning if he holds his tongue. (Proverbs 17: 27-28)

⸎⸎⸎

    As each day passed it became harder for daddy to get around. He needed assistance with everything. He wasn't eating much, and he spent a lot of time in the bed. He began to have difficulty swallowing, and we had to monitor and assist with meals and fluids from fear that daddy would choke. Although we kept him inclined on pillows, Jaclyn and I watched over him vigilantly. We discussed with Tamera the fact that we felt he needed a hospital bed for comfort and safety, and she agreed. Getting daddy in and out of the bed and caring for him was physically taxing on our backs and legs, and my vision was becoming blurred on and off. Jaclyn and I first took the idea to the family. Malcolm wasn't happy about it, but told us if it was what daddy needed he was in agreeance. Raina felt it was too soon, and didn't feel daddy needed a hospital bed in the house just yet. Cadence was angry about the whole idea, and wouldn't discuss it. So we approached momma with the idea. Momma said she wasn't ready for that, so we decided to give her a couple of days to think about it, and approached her with the idea again later.

    Daddy's birthday was finally here, and I was excited and sad at the same time. Excited to celebrate his birthday with him one more time and sad because I was celebrating his birthday with him one last time. I know everything is in God's time, and I was witness to daddy's decline. We had cake and ice cream and while we sang happy birthday to him, Daddy smiled and sang along, "Happy birthday to me." For once I didn't want to hide my tears. I just let them flow, meeting at my chin. Because it was a weekday everyone just stopped by for a couple of hours. No arguments, no nasty looks, just everyone coming together to celebrate an important milestone in daddy's journey.

> Thank you Lord, for another day, tomorrow is not promised to anyone
> Thank you for your precious gift of time
> Forgive me Lord for my shortfalls
> Guide my tongue, may all my words and actions glorify you
> In Jesus name, Amen.

April stopped by for her weekly visit. Once again she spoke to the family about daddy's health and recommended counseling. "There comes a time when it is important for the family to comfort the patient, by letting them know that it's okay to die. That you are okay with the situation. Sometimes a person will try to hold on because their loved one is not at peace, which will cause additional suffering for the entire family."

I remembered the conversation I had with daddy while he was in the hospital. He told me he would be with me always, but I wouldn't be able to see him. I told him I understood and I was okay with that because he would always live in my heart. So daddy knows that I am going to be fine. I told April that daddy and I have already talked, and he knows that I am okay. Everyone else decided to speak to daddy before the day ended except Cadence, she went into a rage. "I will never tell daddy that it's okay for him to die, because it is not okay with me!" Cadence went outside and I followed her hoping to help her find comfort and peace in everything going on.

"Cadence, this is hard for everybody, you need to understand, by telling daddy that you are okay doesn't mean that he will just give up and die. I think this whole process is more for us than daddy. Daddy has already made peace with this, can't you see that. And you not being okay is not going to stop him from dying; it will only break his heart knowing you will have to live the rest of your life with this as unfinished business." Cadence began to cry as I continued to talk. God has the final say, and only he knows what, when and where. Daddy is in hospice, but that doesn't mean any of us will be alive when he leaves this earth. Ask God to help you and he will. There is so much I haven't done yet, Cadence said as she wiped her eyes, and I still need him very much." I took a deep breath and closed my eyes for a moment. "Daddy said his biggest regret in life is when Uncle John passed away and they didn't resolve their issues. The fact is daddy is going to die with or without your permission. I know you don't have issues with daddy, but you need to find some degree of acceptance." I hugged Cadence and went back into the house leaving her to her own thoughts.

> "There is a time for everything, and a season for every activity under heaven; A time to be born and a time to die, a time to plant and a time to uproot, a time to kill and a time to heal, a time to tear down, and a time to build, a time to weep and a time to laugh, a time to mourn and a time to dance, a time to scatter stones and a time to gather them, a time to embrace and a time to refrain, a time to search and a time to give up, a time to keep and a time to throw away, a time to tear and a time to mend, a time to be silent and a time to speak, a time to love and a time to hate, a time for war and a time for peace." (Ecclesiastes 3: 1-8)

Thursday was finally here, and although I prayed for peace, I was prepared to deal with whatever my sisters were dishing out. To my surprise the night went very well. Because Cadence, Raina, Tamera, and Sabrina were spending the night they didn't come over until almost nine o' clock. I figured that was half the battle. Momma and daddy were already in the bed sleeping, and the chores for the day were already done. The girls were dressed and ready for a pajama party. Jaclyn normally slept in the den, and I slept in the living room on the couch. Well not tonight. Raina, Cadence and Sabrina decided that they were going to sleep on the couches in the den, so they could watch movies. Jaclyn and Tamera used the age card and took the two couches in the living room, so I grabbed a sheet and pillow and found a spot on the living room floor. I was beginning to feel a little broken. I have always had a lot of respect for my sisters, and Raina was the sister that I admired the most. I began feeling a sense of loss when it came to my relationships with my siblings. Were my feelings anger because I felt they came in and took over after the work was done, or was I just jealous because of the bond they seemed to share among themselves. Something I used to be a part of but now felt totally left out, unwanted. Knowing that I should never go to sleep with negativity in my heart, I began to talk to God.

> Lord, give me strength
> Continue to mold me, Guide me and help me to grow
> Forgive me, for my selfish thoughts
> Remove the anger from my heart
> I love you Lord, Amen.

The next morning everyone got up happy and cheerful. They dressed for their day and left. After momma dressed daddy he sat on their bed gazing out of the window. I went into the bedroom and sat down beside him, "Hey daddy, I said smiling. He never looked at me; he just continued to stare out of the window. So I didn't say anything else I just sat there beside him looking out of the window as well. Then he spoke, "It's a beautiful day" I looked at him and nodded, "Yes it is daddy, it is a beautiful day." I looked into the sky; it was a beautiful shade of blue, not a cloud in the sky. Although it was autumn, it was unseasonably warm. Their dog Mister was running around the backyard without a care in the world. "Do you see your puppy daddy" he didn't say a word, but I could see he was soaking in all of God's wonders. This is a moment between daddy and God, so I gently rubbed his hand, kissed his forehead and left the room. I went outside to have my moment of peace with God. As I looked up to the sky I could hear the birds chirping, I watched the leaves blow in the summer like breeze. The leaves were starting to change colors, I closed my eyes and felt the warm summer breeze blowing cool against my tears. How could anyone have questions about the existence of God, when everything he created praises him? I feel so grateful for this opportunity God has given me; I began to sing, holding both hands in the air praising God.

It became increasingly difficult to safely feed daddy in the bed, I spoke with Malcolm and told him it was time for a hospital bed. Malcolm agreed, so I told Jaclyn when April comes over I was going to talk to her about bringing a hospital bed into the house. April arrived in the afternoon, and after daddy's assessment I took April, Jaclyn and momma into a room so we could talk. I explained to April that I felt it was time for a hospital bed for daddy. April first looked at Jaclyn and asked her how she felt. Jaclyn nodded her head in agreeance. April then turned to momma. "I know this is very difficult for you Mrs. McCoy, and although Jaclyn and Eliana have been Mr. McCoy's primary caregivers, the final decision is yours." After listening to my reasons why momma agreed. April went into the dining room and proceeded to place the order for the hospital bed. When she finished, she explained to Jaclyn and I that Daddy was in need of other equipment as well, such as and oxygen machine, an aspirator and other items which would help keep daddy comfortable. April then explained daddy's transition was rapidly approaching and we needed to be prepared.

After April left, momma called me into the den and closed the door. "Eliana it's time to make daddy's funeral arrangements. I want you to call and make an appointment. I will momma, how do you want me to handle this, I asked. I don't want you to say anything to anybody; I just want this done now. Okay momma, I responded, I'll do whatever you need." I told Jaclyn what Momma wanted me to do, and she looked at me and said, "Well handle it Eliana." I called the funeral home and made an appointment for the next day, and when Malcolm came I told him what I was instructed to do. I asked him if he wanted to go with me and same as Jaclyn he declined. So the next day when Randy got off of work, we went to the funeral home. Momma gave me specific instructions on what she wanted, and how she wanted it. I followed her requests to the letter. Daddy's request was to be cremated, so after the pickup arrangements were done I only had to pick out an urn for his remains. When I called momma to find out what she wanted she said it didn't matter just choose one. After choosing an urn they asked about an inscription. Once again I called Momma to find out what if any inscription she wanted, and once again she said it didn't matter. So I chose one of daddy's favorites, The Serenity Prayer. We filled out most of daddy death certificate, the program for service, pictures which momma gave me and format. When we left the funeral home I felt relieved I accomplished something for daddy and I didn't have to fight with my sisters over it, knowing that was why momma told me not to tell anybody. I brought the folder home to momma and showed her everything that was done; she was pleased and thanked me. I took the folder to Malcolm and asked if he wanted to go over it, and he told me to put it away, because he didn't need to see anything. After everyone else arrived we cleared the dining room of furniture and waited for the delivery of daddy's bed and equipment. Per the request of my mother, I said nothing to my siblings regarding daddy's funeral arrangements knowing that I would pay for it later on.

> "Therefore put on the full armor of God, so that when the day of evil comes, you may be able to stand your ground, and after you have done everything, to stand. Stand firm then, with the belt of truth buckled around your waist, with the breastplate of righteousness in place, and with your feet fitted with the readiness that comes from the gospel of peace. In addition to all this, take up the shield of faith, with which you can extinguish all the flaming arrows of the evil one. Take the helmet of salvation and the sword of the spirit, which is the word of God. And pray in the spirit on all occasions with all kinds of prayers and requests. With this in mind, be alert and always keep on praying for all the saints." (Ephesians 6: 13-18)

CHAPTER 11

Fight Time

AS THE DAYS continued, I watched daddy decline. He grimaced with most movement. Once he was in the hospital bed he no longer used the bathroom, so daddy needed to be changed regularly. I thought this would be a good opportunity for my brothers to step in and help, but to my surprise they all declined saying they couldn't do it. Tamera told Jaclyn and me she could instruct us on how to properly clean him, but she too couldn't handle this. I found myself emotionally disturbed, I have done everything else without thought, but this was daddy's private space. I went outside to talk this over with God. "Lord, I understand this is a part of life, and it's only the male anatomy, but this is my dad, this is where I came from. My eyes started to water. Then it came to me, this is my journey, my test, my opportunity to stand on God's word. I promised daddy I would be with him through it all, and this is part of all." So, suck it up Eliana, I said to myself, and let your siblings see God's grace and mercy carry you through. So I went into the house and Jaclyn and I changed daddy. He tried to cover himself feeling embarrassed, and that hurt me. I tried to reassure him that I wasn't looking and this had to be done. Once a man, twice a child I said to myself. I did this for my children, so I can do this for daddy as well. Once that was over I felt there wasn't anything I couldn't handle. We had to make sure we turned him every thirty minutes to prevent bed sores, but moving him became very painful for him because of the loss of cartilage between his joints. He spiked a fever on more than one occasion, so the doctor prescribed morphine. April explained the morphine will help with the pain, and allow nature to take its course. My sisters were not handling this well, and boy did it show. Raina and Malcolm decided it was time for a family grieving session. Raina arranged for a minister to be present, and everyone was instructed to attend. I was furious; we were to invite our children so they could take part in this. I spoke to Dahlia about it, but I explained that I refused to participate. I called Pastor Austin in tears. My heart was hurt because I felt that daddy didn't need to hear how everyone felt about him dying while he laid in the next room on display. I wanted to shield him from any emotional pain, and although this was done with good intentions, and it may be good for daddy as well, I wasn't feeling it. Everything my children and grand children feel about me dying should be discussed with me involved or among themselves with the proper counsel. I explained to Pastor Austin I didn't have a problem with the session, but how are you going to talk about how daddy dying makes you feel right in front of him and he isn't even able to participate. What about how this makes him feel. That evening everyone was in attendance, and I stood in the hallway for family prayer, but once they got started with the session, I kissed daddy and told him I would be in the den. I closed the door, and turned on the television. Jaclyn agreed with me, and only went into the dining room to check on daddy. At one point she entered the den upset. "I just checked on daddy and he has tears streaming from his eyes, I just wiped them and told him everything is going to be okay." Pastor Austin came to the house and sat in the den with me; he never said a word, we sat there in silence, until Tamera entered the room. She was crying uncontrollably. This time her tears were all for her son Jacob. Pastor Austin consoled her and we spent our time talking about trials, test, and healing. Before I knew it everyone was leaving and once again I was glad to see them go. Daddy was silent, he didn't say goodnight to anyone, he just smiled and nodded when he was kissed goodbye. The moment the house was silent, daddy started to talk. He was talking to his mother, his brother, and some of his old friends, all of whom preceded him in death. Daddy talked constantly, day and night. I would sit by his bedside and listen to him talk about his home in Georgia, his childhood, the things he loved to eat. The only time he was silent was when there were other people in the house. Jaclyn and I would alternate sitting by his bedside reading scriptures, singing songs or just talking with him. I was trying to take in all of his words, to store them for later when I wouldn't be able to hear his voice. Although I was enjoying daddy's voice there was another voice in the background that was really annoying me. "Eliana, daddy needs something to drink, Eliana, daddy wants to eat, Eliana daddy needs his medicine, Eliana you need to clean daddy's nails, daddy needs to be changed, daddy's mouth is full of mucus and need to be aspirated." An aspirator is a machine with a soft tube used to suck the mucus from the mouth much like what you see in a dentist office. This was necessary because daddy didn't swallow often enough and stood the possibility of choking. It seemed every time Jaclyn or I sat down Raina or Cadence was calling one of us to do something. Why does everything have to be about power and rank, I asked myself? The time and energy it required Raina and Cadence to call Jaclyn or myself to do something for daddy is far more than the energy required to take care of it themselves. But instead of fighting about it, I held my tongue and did whatever was asked of me. They weren't asking me to do anything for them. Actually they never asked anyway, but regardless it was all for daddy.

> "Let love and faithfulness never leave you; bind them around your neck, write them on the tablet of your heart. Then you will win favor and a good name in the sight of God and man." (Proverbs 3: 3-4)

It became visible to almost everyone that the sun was setting on daddy's journey in life. Everyone began to spend more time at the house. Although I was feeling like the hired help, with my decision to hold my tongue there was more peace in the house. Once again my sisters decided to spend the night, except this time they came early. Everyone was on edge feeling daddy could leave any minute now. Momma and Raina were in the living room with daddy giving him ensure to drink. Tamera, Cadence and I were in the kitchen and Jaclyn was sitting in the den. Cadence and Tamer started to argue. I wasn't paying attention to what was being said until Tamera called Cadence out of her name. Cadence flew into a rage, Jaclyn ran into the kitchen just in time to see the chair fly across the room as Cadence tried to get to Tamera. I ran to Tamera's side to block her from getting to Cadence and Jaclyn grabbed Cadence and moved her into the hallway. Raina ran into the kitchen screaming, "What in the world is going on here, what are you doing, Daddy is dying and you guys want to fight!" Cadence was screaming at Tamera as Jaclyn moved her into another room, and Tamera stood there calmly waiting for Cadence to get close enough for her to hit. Raina started crying, "I'm calling Malcolm right now!" Those words seemed to calm the entire situation and everyone sat down. Tamera went into the dining room to be with daddy, and Cadence went back into the kitchen with Jaclyn so they could talk about what happened. I walked into the dining room to check on daddy and Tamera was aspirating daddy's mouth, but daddy was fighting her. He looked very distressed. When I asked Tamera what was wrong, daddy reached out his hand to me. I started to scream at Tamera, "What are you doing, stop you're hurting him!" As I reached for her hand Tamera pushed my hand away, "Raina gave him ensure to drink and he wasn't swallowing it, I'm just trying to get it all out!" I continued to scream at her, "You're hurting him Tamera, stop please! Eliana, if you can't take it you need to leave the room." I grabbed her hand, and she pushed my hand away, so I walked over to the plug and unplugged the machine, "I said stop it now!" Tamera put the tube down and walked into the kitchen. After I calmed daddy I went into the kitchen to talk to Tamera. "I know you were helping daddy, but you were hurting him and you needed to stop. Tamera looked at me with tears in her eyes, "I was removing the fluid from daddy's mouth so he wouldn't choke. I know what I'm doing I handle patients all the time! This is not a patient, I screamed, this is daddy!! Tamera dropped her head down and started to sob. "Don't you think I know who he is? I would never hurt him, and how dare you treat me like I was." Jaclyn walked over to me, "Eliana you are totally out of order, how dare you speak to Tamera in that manner, that was mean and hateful, and you need to apologize to her for that. You weren't in the room Jaclyn, so you didn't see what I saw. I know Tamera was helping, but she was too emotional from arguing with Cadence, she was too rough and she needed to stop for a moment, that's all I wanted." I was out done. Here I stand arguing with the one person that stood with me through this entire ordeal. I was too angry to cry, and too hurt to talk about it any further so I sat in a chair with my arms folded, refusing to say another word period.

Moments later Raina went outside, and returned saying Malcolm was here. Everyone went outside to talk to Malcolm. I could hear them all talking, and I assumed everyone was pleading their case to him. I just sat there in the kitchen staring at the wall.

> Lord, help us, this house is out of order, and everyone is out of control
> Give me peace in my heart, forgive me Lord
> I am trying to maintain composure, hold my tongue
> Help me, to think before I speak, Give me the words to say
> In Jesus name, Amen.

After hearing the side door close Malcolm entered the room. He appeared at ease, but had a look of authority on his face. "Eliana it is necessary for everyone to get along, you girls can't fight, that's just wrong." I never looked at him, my arms still folded. I only continued to stare ahead while Malcolm continued to speak. "Momma and Daddy need peace and I expect everyone involved to cooperate. You girls can't run around screaming at each other, what about their neighbors Eliana, this cannot happen again Okay?" I looked at him and replied, "Yea, okay" Malcolm turned and walked away. I could hear everyone outside talking and laughing. I thought to myself Rod Sterling must be near because I'm in the twilight zone. I got up and found a spot on the living room floor, rolled in my sheet promising not to get up until everyone was gone. The next morning everyone got up and dressed for work, talking as though nothing ever happened. I didn't wake up with the attitude I went to sleep with. I went to daddy's bedside and kissed his forehead. "Good morning Daddy, one thing is for sure, they will definitely keep me on my knees praying. I just wish I didn't have to repent so much." Daddy just smiled and continued his conversation with his dead mother and Uncle John.

After every one was gone Jaclyn and I sat down to talk about everything that happened. She was very angry with me, because she felt I attacked Tamera, and Tamera is fragile emotionally after losing Jacob. I explained to her that I wasn't attacking Tamera I just wanted her to stop and take a break or something. The entire house was in turmoil and out of control. I told Jaclyn I would apologize to Tamera when I talk to her. We hugged and resumed our duties as caregivers.

Once a week, Jaclyn and I would go home for a night or two; so we could spend quality time with our husbands. We didn't go at the same time so someone was always there with momma and daddy around the clock. It was Jaclyn's turn to go home and I assured her that I would call her if anything happened.

Daddy's pain was becoming increasingly worse, and the pain my sisters were causing me was equal. They would call me to give daddy his medicine, and then want to check to make sure I was giving him the right amount. So I started asking them how they wanted me to do things, that made them happy, and I'm sure they knew only God could keep me quiet, so all glory to God. It seemed to hurt daddy to touch him, and he was no longer eating at all. While I was changing him I noticed his urine looked thick and slimy. I called Tamera in and showed her. "Daddy is in renal failure, that's why his urine looks that way," she said shaking her head. "Why Tamera" I asked. "Eliana, all of his organs are starting to shut down. Look at his skin, it's a little yellow, well that's his liver. This is just the process; his organs will shut down until his heart finally stops. I closed my eyes and asked Tamera, what can we do? She hugged me, just continue to make daddy as comfortable as possible. We were using the moist mouth sponges to give him fluids. Every time I looked at daddy he appeared to be suffering. So I sat down at daddy's bedside to read some bible verses to him and when I finished I held his hand and prayed.

> Lord,
> I ask that you open your loving arms, and accept this man into your kingdom
> For he is weak, he is weary, and he is worn
> I love him Lord, but you love him more
> Thank you for blessing me, with this wonderful man
> I love you Lord
> And I thank you for your Grace and Mercy
> In Jesus name, Amen.

After daddy and I prayed, I looked into his eyes and spoke to him. I love you daddy, and I want you to know that it's okay to go with God. There is no need to stay just because some of us aren't ready to say goodbye. We will look after momma; we will always see that she is okay. I will stay by your side until it's time for you to go. I will walk with you to the end of your journey here knowing that once you are absent from your body you will be with our God. It hurts me daddy to watch you suffer so I ask God to give you peace in your heart and mind. You promised me that you would be with me always, and I promise you that I will be with you. I love you daddy, but God loves you more. Daddy looked at me and smiled, I knew he was okay. I leaned over and kissed daddy gently on his lips knowing his journey here with me would soon be over.

> "Come to me, all you who are weary and burdened, and I will give you rest. Take my yoke upon you and learn from me, for I

am gentle and humble in heart, and you will find rest for your souls. For my yoke is easy and my burden is light." (Matthew 11: 28-30)

Dahlia stopped by for her usual visit. I was really happy to see her; Dahlia was such a breath of fresh air. While we were talking she told me she talked with grand daddy today. He told her not to be angry, and he would be leaving around seven-fifteen. I couldn't explain that, but we laughed about how he always called her Barbara. Funny how such a minor thing could cause laughter. It became our private joke. I was especially thankful this day for Dahlia, because I felt surrounded by people that didn't like me, by my own choice of course. I wouldn't leave, I couldn't break my word, and daddy always said a person is only as good as their word. Before Dahlia left I got all the hugs I could, because I knew once she left the fun was over. Randy was still coming by after work, but he was having difficulty coming into the house to see daddy. He was having a hard time because he cared for his father before he died while he was home. So when Randy would visit we would sit outside or go for walks. He was my sounding board; he listened to all my complaints, beefs, and concerns. We laughed, and we cried together, or he would just hold me in silence just because. The rest of the day went quite well. I often found myself looking around repeating daddy's words, "It's a beautiful day." Thank you Lord for peace.

Daddy spent the night as usual talking about everything under the sun, as I lay on the couch listening. By morning daddy stopped talking. The house was unusually silent. I walked over to daddy's bedside and looked at him. His eyes met mine and he said, "Hi Eliana." It wasn't often that daddy said names. Although he knew we were his children he didn't remember us by name. Every now and then he would call someone's name, but the way he smiled at me always implied to me that he knew who I was and I was good with that. "Good morning Daddy, I said with a big smile, "Looks like it's going to be another beautiful day." The music was playing, and I started to sing while I straightened up. I noticed how odd it was that daddy stopped talking as though he said everything that he needed to say. I cleaned daddy up, and prepared him for his day. Today I felt odd, but I assumed it was daddy's silence and continued with my daily chores. In the afternoon Cadence and Raina came to spend time with daddy. After kissing him hello, Raina looked at daddy and said, "Daddy you don't want Eliana in here do you. Tell Eliana to leave." Daddy just shook his head, and then he smiled at her. Raina continued, "Eliana needs to leave the room doesn't she daddy." So I leaned over and kissed daddy on his forehead and whispered as I glared at Raina, "I'll be right in the den daddy, just call me if you need me." I went into the den and sat down on the couch once again speaking out loud. "Why does she have to be this way with me Lord? I'm trying so very hard not to say anything. I don't want to fight anymore." At that moment I heard Raina saying, "What's wrong daddy? Her next words were, "Eliana something is wrong with daddy!" As I got up momma hurried pass me into the dining room. I approached daddy's bedside, daddy was moving he head back and forth looking around. First he looked at momma, then Cadence, then Raina, next his eyes met mine, and he smiled and closed his eyes. Daddy started to sweat, but I could clearly see that he had lost consciousness. Cadence and Raina were panicked and screaming at me. "Do something Eliana, call for help!" I went to the bathroom and returned with a cool damp cloth, and I started to rub daddy forehead. "There isn't anything to do, I calmly said, "Nature just has to take its course. No! Raina screamed, call April now! I thought if I remained calm everyone else would be as well, but I was wrong. Cadence was standing by daddy rubbing his hand crying. Raina was in a frenzy. I raised my voice and spoke again, "Raina, I said there isn't anything that we can do. Momma signed a DNR form, so no one will perform life saving techniques. He is in hospice, and making his transition from this life, so say what you need to say to him, tell him you love him, because there's nothing left to do except wait!" Once daddy stopped sweating he appeared to be in a deep sleep. As I turned to walk away Raina stepped in front of me, "okay Eliana, I understand that daddy is in hospice, but you still need to call April." I had just used the last of my patience with my sister and I was no longer speaking calmly. "Raina, if you want April called, the hospice book is sitting right over there, pick up the phone and call her yourself!" I walked into the den and picked up my phone to call Jaclyn, and Tamera to let them know what was going on with daddy. Raina picked up the book with a look of disgust, and called April. Once April arrived she examined daddy and confirmed what I said earlier. Riana's complaint was daddy looked as though he was struggling to breathe, so April suggested that we put the oxygen on daddy, she said that would probably make him more comfortable. Momma agreed so Raina and I pulled out the machine and put the oxygen tube on daddy's face. He did seem to relax, not breathing as hard, and that made Raina feel a little better. Before April left she came to me and told me it was time to call the whole family, so they could spend time with daddy before his transition, so I went to the phone and called my siblings letting them know that it's time.

Everyone arrived in a timely manner. One by one coming to daddy bedside to talk to him. When Tamera arrived she checked daddy's eyes, "His pupils are fixed and dilated Eliana" then she checked his blood pressure, fifty-two over thirty-eight, she shook her head, "Yes it's time."

> "I will praise you, O Lord, with all my heart, I will tell of all your wonders. I will be glad and rejoice in you; I will sing praise to your name, O most high." (Psalms 9: 1-2)

CHAPTER **12**

Time to Say Goodbye

ONCE JACLYN ARRIVED, she walked to Daddy's bedside and started to pray. When she finished I told her daddy's stats, and explained it's just a matter of time. Jaclyn sat down in a chair, as I stood by daddy's bedside Sabrina walked into the dining room. "Hey everybody" she said, she spoke as though nothing was wrong. "Hey Sabrina" I replied, "As you can see daddy has lost consciousness, his pupils are fixed and dilated, and his blood pressure is about fifty over thirty-eight." Sabrina looked at daddy; she leaned over and kissed him. She turned to us with a look of confusion on her face, "You guys are standing around looking grim, but Daddy is going to be alright. What did you just say, Jaclyn asked her? My mouth dropped, as I stared at Sabrina bewildered. She said it again, "Daddy will be alright, you'll see." Thanksgiving he'll be sitting in the den with us watching TV. You can't be serious, I said slightly irritated. You're telling me that this man, as I pointed to daddy, that's laying there in a coma, is going to be sitting in the den with you six weeks from now watching TV? Sabrina replied, yes that's exactly what I'm saying! I stood there looking at Sabrina wondering what part of her brain had to shut down in order for her to believe this. Jaclyn looked at Sabrina and I could tell she was quite angry. "Sabrina, what you just said is stupid, you're stupid. Don't talk to me anymore; just don't say another word to me. Sabrina, I said calmly, the only way that daddy is going to be in the den with you on thanksgiving is in spirit, you need to get a grip on reality, and talk to somebody." Sabrina walked into the den to talk with everyone else.

From that point the house was very busy. Most of our children came by to visit. Someone was by daddy's bedside at all times. We could visibly see that daddy's body was changing. His skin started to break down, very thin and easy to tear. No movement just the sound of the oxygen machine and our voices. Saturday night Tamera, Cadence and Raina stayed at the house with Jaclyn, momma and me. As I sat on the couch reading my bible, Cadence sat by daddy's bedside holding his hand talking to him. I asked God, please help her find peace with this, she is hurting and for her own sake she needs that.

Jaclyn, Tamera, and I got up early the next morning to wash daddy and start the day. Daddy's skin looked bad, and I was amazed at how that could happen in such a short period of time. He looked like a skeleton, his skin was yellow and he had developed sores. When we finished Jaclyn and I went into the basement to talk about it, then Tamera came down. "Daddy's body is breaking down, and once I thought about it this is happening because he is still on the oxygen. We need to turn the oxygen off. What does the oxygen have to do with this Tamera; he didn't look like this before? Tamera held my hands, the machine is feeding oxygen to his brain and it's just enough to keep his lungs going and his heart beating. Jaclyn spoke, so you're telling us that the oxygen is only keeping those organs going? Yes, Tamera said, and to be frank about it if we don't turn the oxygen off we will witness an awful sight physically. I didn't say anything to Raina or Cadence, they wouldn't understand, and there are a lot of things I didn't tell them because of that. You don't need to talk to them about it either, because they are too emotional and wouldn't understand the medical aspect of anything, and I can't talk to them about it either, because nothing I say would matter. I thought for a moment then I spoke, in other words daddy is decomposing before our eyes. Eliana, that is the one thing you never want to see, but the answer to your question is yes. No one knows all about the human body, but his other organs have already shut down, with the oxygen he may live another couple of hours or days maybe even, but his skin will tear every time you touch him, and the sight of his body will be in your mind forever. Tamera looked at Jaclyn and said, I've already told momma she said okay, so we need to turn the oxygen off. Jaclyn looked at me and I shook my head yes, we need to turn it off.

So we went upstairs to tell Raina and Cadence. They were in the room at daddy's bedside. As I walked in; I heard the machine beep as it turned off. Raina screamed, what is going on! Tamera just turned the oxygen off, I replied. Oh no! She can't do that! Raina got up and headed for the machine which was in the front hallway. You can't turn that off daddy needs that, she turned the machine back on. April said the oxygen would make him more comfortable. Tamera replied in a very compassionate tone, he doesn't need the oxygen any more, his body is breaking down and it's time to turn it off. She reached down and shut the power off again. Raina turned it back on. I'm telling you don't turn it off again Tamera! And Raina went back into the dining room to talk to cadence. As I stood in the dining room I once again heard the machine beep.

"That's it!" Raina screamed as she ran into the hallway to stop Tamera. I could hear them arguing back and forth, and then I heard the machine beep as it came back on. Raina came back into the dining room, and I turned to her. Raina, it's time to turn the machine off. Raina was enraged by my words, I am so sick of this, and I am sick of you guys coming in here and doing whatever you want, I'm leaving! Jaclyn looked at Raina and said, get out then! Raina turned to Jaclyn, what did you just say to me? I said get out! If you want to leave then leave, nobody's stopping you from going, and I guarantee you won't be missed, so just get your things and get out! At that time Tamera was coming out of momma's bedroom with momma in tow. Momma stood there looked at all of her daughters and said' "Turn the machine off" she turned and walked back into her bedroom and pushed the door closed. Cadence started to cry, as Tamera walked into the front hallway for the last time and unplugged the oxygen machine. The machine beeped and Riana's eyes began to water, I'm calling Malcolm! She screamed, and she went out the side door. Tamera said I'll go and talk to her, and she too went outside to talk to Raina. The next thing I knew I could hear screaming coming from outside. It was Tamera and Raina, so Jaclyn went out to try and defuse the situation. I ran to the living room window to look and could not believe my eyes. Raina was throwing her keys onto the ground and as she was stepping towards Tamera who was standing there waiting for Raina to get close enough, Jaclyn stepped in between the two. She pushed Raina away and told Tamera to go in the house. Raina started crying, and Tamera still didn't move. Jaclyn turned and pointed to Tamera, I said go in the house now! Tamera turned and walked away. Jaclyn stood outside talking to Raina for a couple of minutes then she returned into the house. I could see Raina on her cell phone as I got up from the couch. I walked into momma's bedroom and asked her if she was okay, but before she could answer me I heard the side door slam shut. It was Malcolm, and he was furious. I walked into the dining room to hear what he had to say. He pointed to Jaclyn and me and said you all are out of order; you have no right to make any decisions without first discussing it with everyone. I just stood there in shock, but as I felt my heart ache I was overcome by anger. While Malcolm stood there fussing at Jaclyn and me, I was deep in thought. How could he just take Riana's word and come in here to reprimand us. Why didn't he just ask what happened? Then I remembered his words to us, "If anything happened to daddy I would be crazy." Well he was right; Malcolm was behaving like he lost it. When he finished fussing he sat down on the piano bench in the dining room and shouted, "And turn that music off! Okay, fine I'll turn the music off!" From the time hospice began for daddy we played his favorite gospel music all day, and during the last week the music played around the clock. I walked into the living room and pushed the power button. "Well Jesus, I whispered, I guess they want you to step outside for a little while, oh well as they all say, stupid is as stupid does, I shook my head in despair over my family. The house was filled with silence. A painful kind of silence. I walked into momma's bedroom and pushed the door up trying to shake off all of the things I was currently feeling. As I stood there I could hear Raina and Cadence talking with Malcolm about daddy's funeral. Raina was saying, "We will have to do an obituary, and because daddy's being cremated, do we put an urn on top of a casket during the service." I closed my eyes, Lord is she for real, daddy hasn't even stopped breathing and now she sits at his bedside making his funeral arrangements. Before I walked into the dining room, I asked God to forgive me for any pleasure I may receive from this. I looked at Raina and in a smug tone, "You don't even have to worry about that. What do you mean by that Eliana, she asked. What I mean is it's been taken care of. What's been taken care of, her voice was once again raised. What I mean is his funeral arrangements have been taken care of, so you don't have to worry about that! Raina looked at me eyes ablaze, who took care of daddy's funeral arrangements! I did, I said, still remaining calm, I made the arrangements. You made daddy's funeral arrangements and you didn't say anything to anybody, just who do you think you are Eliana, you had no right to do that without talking to us about it first! I could see Malcolm out of the corner of my eyes, he didn't move, nor did he say a word. I thought to myself, Malcolm you wimp, how could you just sit there and say nothing knowing there would be a lot of bad feelings to come from this. You could have nipped this in the bud, by telling them that you knew about it, and I was only doing as I was told. Perhaps he is too grief stricken to speak, nevertheless, I was growing very tired of dealing with everyone's foolishness, meanwhile Raina continued to fuss, so I just cut her off. "Enough already, it's done, no obituary, the pictures, the urn, the program, everything is already done and the only things we don't know is his date of death and time of service. By the time I finished speaking Raina was glaring at me, and I could tell she was outdone. While she was still expressing her opinion to me, I turned and walked away feeling relieved of some of the pressure I was feeling. I am so done with these people I said to myself aloud. Lord

just give me the strength to deal with them just a little while longer.
"I consider that our present sufferings are not worth comparing with the glory that will be revealed in us." (Romans 8: 18)

"And we know that in all things God works for the good of those who love him, who have been called according to his purpose. For those God foreknew he also predestined to be conformed to the likeness of his son, that he might be the firstborn among many brothers. And those he predestined, he also called, those he called, he also justified, those he justified, he also glorified." (Romans 8: 28-30)

After I showered and dressed, I went back into the basement, the only place in this house that I could have solitude. I was sitting in a chair reading my scriptures when I heard footsteps. As I turned I saw Cadence walking towards me. She didn't look angry or upset, just confused. "Eliana I just want to know what's going with daddy, she spoke softly. Daddy's dying Cadence that is what's going on with daddy. Look Eliana, she said, I don't understand, everybody is real upset with you right now, and I want to give you an opportunity to help me understand. Look I said sharply, we all knew this was coming; April said this was going to happen. Cadence tone changed, what did April say Eliana? She said a lot of thing, I began to feel uncomfortable. Every time daddy's condition changed she told us. I understand that, but why didn't you tell us? This was coming from the woman who refused to tell daddy it was okay to die, even if his continuance would cause him to suffer. I could hear Tamera's words, "Some things are best left unsaid, they won't listen anyway, and anything you say won't matter." After taking a minute I spoke. "Cadence, you guys wouldn't listen to anything that I had to say because you guys know everything and I know nothing." Cadence turned around and walked away, and knowing Cadence as I thought I did, she was going upstairs to discuss this with Raina and I was sure by the time they were through this would just be one more thing to fight with me about. God's saving grace is my time spent here was quickly coming to a close. "I will keep my promise daddy, I said aloud. You told me not to leave, and I won't leave until I have done all that I am suppose to do." When Jaclyn came into the basement I asked her, why do they have to be this way? Jaclyn looked at me and replied, "They hated Jesus, and he did nothing, why not you? Jesus carried his cross, so pick up your cross Eliana, and follow him: I could hear Randy saying, "I say it's time to pray."

"But I tell you; Love your enemies and pray for those who persecute you," (Matthew 5: 44)

Jaclyn and I decided to spend the rest of the day in the basement. Although I could hear my family upstairs, it was quiet and very peaceful. We were in the middle of reading bible scriptures when Tamera shouted down the stairs, "Jaclyn, Eliana, come quick, I want you to see something!" Jaclyn and I jumped up from our chairs and ran for the stairs. Her voice wasn't panicked so I knew daddy was still here, but as I ran up the stairs I wondered, what miracle does God have for me to witness.

As I entered the dining room the blinds were opened and the sun was beaming through the side and the front of the house. The dining room light was on, so the room seemed exceptionally bright. Tamera walked over to his bedside and pointed at daddy, "Look at him" she said. As I stood at the foot of daddy's bed he appeared to be glowing. Jaclyn said, "That's from the light and the baby oil you put on him. Tamera replied, I didn't put any oil on daddy, I didn't do anything." Daddy's skin was glistening as he laid there in a peaceful sleep, Tamera walked over and turned the light off, and the glow was obvious, the sun was shining like a beam through the window directly on daddy's body, his body glistening, in combination with the color of his skin daddy was aglow. "This is beautiful; I said aloud, he looks as though he is truly ready. Standing at the foot of his bed the sunlight was beaming on his whole body in a stream of light, it looked as though God had opened the windows of heaven to welcome daddy. We stood there in amazement looking daddy. I held his feet, closed my eyes and started to pray silently.

> My father, which art in heaven
> Thank you, for answering my prayers, for giving me strength
> Thank you Lord, for blessing this man, with your grace and tender mercies
> Thank you Lord, for blessing me with this man, my Daddy
> Bless my family with the strength they will need to endure
> Give them peace that surpasses all understanding, and love that can only come from you
> I pray that there is something that I have said or done during this time
> That will draw my family closer to you, I love you Lord, and I thank you
> For being God, perfect in every way, allowing me this test,
> Giving me this witness as my testimony, I will always sing praise to your holy name
> In Jesus name I pray, Amen.

As I released daddy's feet I looked around the room, the house was quiet except the voices of my sisters and brothers coming from the den. I thought to myself, Lord, now more than ever we should be praying together. We should be celebrating daddy's life and the transition yet to come. The music should be playing and we should be singing with thanksgiving and praises to our Lord and Savior on this glorious day that he has blessed us with. I lowered my head and whispered, "The way everyone is right now I'm sure that's just not going to happen."

I went back into the basement to resume my studies, but I was overcome by emotions. As I sat in the chair I began to talk to God, "April was right Lord, death does bring out the worst in some families, and we are living proof of that. The last thirty days has been filled with arguments and fights, and lots of he said and she did. Daddy kept us together, daddy kept the peace, but does that have to mean no daddy therefore no peace? Then the Holy Spirit spoke to my heart. "You Eliana have made this about you and your feelings. This is not about you; this is about God and his glory. You want your family to see the Jesus in you, yet you are in the basement where you can be seen by no one. God's grace and mercy gave you the strength to get through this, and yet you hide, you have never been alone, and if you look to the ground you will only see my set of footprints in the sand, because I am carrying you. Continue to praise God for the entire world to see." I started to cry, because I felt like I had fallen short once again. "Forgive me Lord, I love you." And I closed my books and went upstairs to be with my family. By the time I got upstairs everyone was eating dinner. I made my plate and sat down, but no one would talk to me. I walked over to daddy's bedside the glow was gone. I looked at him and said, "Daddy, my work here is done."

    I went into the den and gathered my belongings, packed my clothes and called Randy to come and get me. I went into momma's bedroom and closed the door; she was sitting on her bed. "Momma, I'm going home now. You're really going home Eliana, she asked? Momma looked sad, Yes momma, I have done all that I could. Daddy is resting now, and there is nothing else left to do except wait. When are you coming back, she asked? I talked to Tamera and she is going to stay tonight, and she said she would call when daddy makes his transition, and as soon as someone calls me, I'll be back. I need to go home now and be with my husband. Thank you Eliana, she said softly, you're very welcome Momma, I kissed her on her cheek, and I went into the kitchen to wait for Randy to show.

ᴊᴊᴊ

    I was so very happy to be back at home, although filled with emotions, I had my prayer partner, my confidant, and my best friend back by my side, his embrace shielding me from the world. Through all of the confusion I had forgotten how wonderful and peaceful my home was. My wonderful husband, loving children, and even my grand children, I truly had a new appreciation for my life now. After spending quality time with Randy and the family, I felt totally drained and retired to bed for the night. Although I closed my eyes I laid there waiting for the telephone to ring. I opened my eyes and looked at the clock it was five am, my first thought was to just get dressed and go over to my parents house, my next thought was Tamera's words to me before I left the house, "Eliana, this could take hours, go home and get some rest, I promise I'll call you, or I'll see you in the morning." Without realizing I had dosed off to sleep I was awakened by the sound of the telephone ringing. It was Malcolm, he sounded very calm, "Morning Eliana, I'm calling to let you know that daddy has made his transition. I closed my eyes, okay, I'll be right over. Take your time Eliana, don't hurt yourself, we will see you as soon as you get here.

> "No one lights a lamp and puts it in a place where it will be hidden, or under a bowl. Instead he puts it on its stand, so that those who come in may see the light. Your eye is the lamp of your body. When your eyes are good, your whole body also is full of light, but when they are bad, your body also is full of darkness. Therefore, if your whole body is full of light, and no part of it dark, it will be completely lighted, as when the light of a lamp shines on you." (Luke 11: 33-36)

Once I arrived at my parent's house, I noticed everyone's cars were there. With everyone's travel time I could tell that they waited for everyone else to arrive before calling me. As I walked into the house I could hear the pinball machine in the basement, and I safely assumed that Shamar was down there. I could see April standing in the hallway, Malcolm met me in the hallway before I could enter the dining room, "Did you call the funeral home, I asked Malcolm? No, I didn't, he replied. I walked into the dining room everyone was standing around daddy, I walked over to daddy, his eyes were open, but empty. "This was only his house, I said aloud. I put my hands over his eyes to close them, but they were too dry. I approached April to get the information for daddy's paperwork. She told me she pronounced him dead about seven-fifteen am, she wrote down for me everything I would need to provide to the funeral home, she offered her condolences to the family, provided us with information on grief counseling and left. I asked Malcolm, "Why didn't you call the funeral home to come and get daddy? We were waiting for you to get here and do it, he replied. So I walked into my parent's bedroom and made arrangements for daddy to be picked up. They said it would be a couple of hours so we had a little time to get ready.

Unlike all the days prior, which were sunny and warm, today was rainy and cool. I went outside to call Becky and let her know that daddy had passed away. After some much needed time spent with Becky, I knew it was time to go into the house to get things in order. I went into the dining room and said, "Okay everybody, the funeral home will be here soon, so we need to move the equipment and clear daddy's bed. Moments later Raina came into the house saying, the funeral home is here." Wade was busy moving the equipment out of the way. Mr. Smith introduced himself when he came in. He then asked the family to leave the room, because this is a difficult thing to handle. Sabrina and Malcolm went into the den, Riana's friend the Pastor took Momma into her bedroom and closed the door, Shamar stayed in the basement, and Raina and her husband went outside, while Randy sat in the kitchen. Tamera's best friend Katherine was there, Tamera and I both told Mr. Smith that we were okay and will help prepare daddy's body for transport. Cadence stood in the hallway saying she was okay and she was not leaving. We started taking everything off of the bed when Tamera fell to her knees at daddy's bedside, I asked Katherine to take Tamera out of the room. We pulled the sides of the sheets up to wrap daddy and Cadence started screaming, "Don't cover up my daddy's face! She was crying hysterically. Mr. Smith apologized, but demanded everyone leave the room. Malcolm came in and took Cadence into the den and closed the door. Mr. Smith turned around and looked at me but before he could speak I spoke, "Look, I said, I am okay, I know you have a job to do, but I promised my dad I would see this to the end. Just look in my eyes, I'm telling you I can handle this, for me this is the easy part, this is only where God housed my dad." Mr. Smith looked at me for a minute and replied, are you sure you'll be okay? Let's do this, I responded. So we wrapped daddy in his sheet and put him in the body bag on the gurney. We strapped him down and out the front door they went. I followed daddy's body to the truck and as they were closing the back door I said aloud, "I'll see you on the other side daddy."

> "Where O death is your victory? Where o death is your sting? The sting of death is sin, and the power of sin is the law. But thanks be to God! He gives us victory through our Lord Jesus Christ. Therefore, my dear brothers, stand firm. Let nothing move you. Always give yourselves fully to the work of the Lord, because you know that your labor in the Lord is not in vain." (1 Corinthians 15: 55-58)

Preparing for daddy's funeral was not as difficult as I thought it would be; but dealing with the living; my siblings left much to desire. I noticed Randy did not seem like himself. He was not as compassionate or empathetic as usual, I didn't quite understand, but I knew this was something I would have to address later.

The day of the funeral was beautiful, Sunny and warm, for a day in October. After prayer Randy and I got in our car to drive to the funeral home. Randy got confused and I had to give him directions there. I found myself agitated that he couldn't find his way somewhere we have been a countless number of times. Once we arrived at the funeral home, as we waited to go in I could feel the anxiety. "This is it, I said to myself, the final step, closure, Daddy is really gone. My go-to-person is gone. Then I remembered what Pastor Austin told me, "A persons childhood ends when their parents die." I looked at my mother, momma is still here, but we never had that type of relationship, I never tried to have that with momma, because I always had daddy. Well it's never too late to start, I said to myself. I looked up to the sky, "Right now Lord, I feel bare, naked, and exposed. Help me through this day Lord. The tears began to fall, I held Randy's hand tight, hoping and praying that this day would be over soon.

What does a caregiver do, after the person being cared for dies? Randy and Dahlia were working during the day. It was time for God and me to deal with my emotions.

CHAPTER **13**

After Goodbye

PREPARING FOR THE holidays was enough to occupy some of my time, but I felt hurt and angry, betrayed by my family. All of the things that daddy taught us didn't apply when we needed it most, when he was dying. I needed time to evaluate myself. I was angry that daddy spent my whole life building a family structure that we managed to destroy in one month. We were no longer friends and I was disappointed that we couldn't stick together through this time of grief. I felt mistreated, and abused, how could they treat me this way all in the name of love. But they weren't the only guilty party; knowing that I too didn't do everything that I could have to maintain peace within the family unit, because I expected Malcolm to do that. Then I realized; Daddy was not the only one going through a transition, we have all experienced a transition into a life that did not include his presence. I felt I needed time to heal, time to forgive, and time away from my family. I could hear Randy say, "Eliana it's time to pray."

> Lord, Thank you for never leaving me alone
> Forgive my trespasses, as I forgive those who trespass against me
> Thank you Lord, for loving me, and showing me how I used to be before I applied your word to my life
> Bless my home and my family

Bless my Mother and my siblings with understanding and wisdom
Give them peace in their hearts
I feel like Joseph having been thrown in the pit, Guide me Lord
You have designed a path for me, and I will follow you all the days of my life
I love you Lord, Amen.

As I awoke every morning, I used my newly found appreciation for the beauty of every day by taking time to look outside at God's creation. Daddy loved the outdoors, and now I can see things a little different. I now watch in great detail the miracle of how the seasons change. Being back at home allowed me opportunity to get some much needed rest. I was once again receiving steroid infusions after having an ms relapse shortly after daddy's memorial service. I was using my walker to get around, but it didn't slow me down. Something was going on with Randy. He seemed different, not sure of himself, and whenever I mentioned it to him he became quite defensive.

Although we didn't talk to Randy Jr. we still spent time with his children. We always agreed whatever drama adults experience; it should never affect the children. Randy Jr. would drop the boys off or pick them up, but he would never get out of the car. How could I blame him, each time he came to drop the boys off, I never said a word, nor did I invite him into the house. This weekend Randy and I went to the house to pick up Samuel and Phillip for the weekend, and Nadia, Rand's wife asked me how we were doing. So without going into detail I explained my father just passed away. "Oh my goodness Eliana, I am so sorry, she said, why didn't you tell us." I felt this was an opportunity to express myself, "Why would I bother to tell you about my dad when you guys don't care, it wouldn't have mattered, it's not like you were going to be there anyway, I responded." Nadia sat there looking at me surprised, I didn't say another word, after doing to Nadia what my family did to me. I was immediately sorry, but said nothing; I just helped her get the boys ready so we could have some quality time together. On the ride home I realized how ridicules this situation is, and I'm not making things any easier behaving like a homemade fool. Enough is enough, this must come to a close, I then decided, the next time Randy Jr comes to the house to drop off the boys we are going to talk.

The weekend was uneventful, but Randy was distant with the children. He didn't play with the children like he normally did, and seemed a little agitated if Phillip cried. He didn't have much to say the whole weekend. My first thought was perhaps he was upset because I left home to care for my father; my next thought was he was upset because I came home. Randy and I have always talked about everything, and this too will be up for discussion soon.

> "Be wise in the way you act toward outsiders, make the most of every opportunity. Let your conversation be always full of grace, seasoned with salt, so that you may know how to answer everyone. (Colossians 4: 5-6)

Thanksgiving came and went; things were very different for me. Not only was this my first thanksgiving without daddy, but this was my first thanksgiving without my family. Except for my mother, Jaclyn, and Tamera I hadn't talked to any of my family since daddy's memorial service, I didn't have any desire to see or speak to any of them. Jaclyn and her family spent thanksgiving with me and my family excluding Randy Jr. and the kids, but I trusted God was working that out. We had good food, fun, and fellowship, and although I missed daddy's presence his words play over in my mind, "Eliana I will be with you always, but you won't be able to see me." I thank God for such a wonderful opportunity and experience. So the day was enjoyable, although with daddy gone I knew everything about the holidays would be a little hard the first time around.

A few days following thanksgiving while I was planning my Christmas dinner the telephone rang, reluctant I answered it. It was my sister Sabrina and she was angry.

Without any small talk, she cut to the chase, "Eliana, where were you thanksgiving, everyone was present and you were a no show." The tone of her voice irritated me. "What was the problem Sabrina the turkey you guys cooked wasn't big enough to roast so you missed me, I responded surly. I am no longer available for foolishness, thanks for the invite, but I'll pass. You can't pass, her voice was raised, see Eliana you think you are so smart, you make a decision and choose to stick with it no matter what, that is no way to live. Just like your job, you said you wouldn't leave until you were ready. Just because you made up your mind doesn't mean it had to turn out that way." Listening to Sabrina fuss, I had a sudden flashback, and once again I was angry. "Listen Sabrina, it didn't have to work out that way but it did. I don't have a problem with divine order, and I am willing to accept whatever God has planned for me. What I choose is not to be around people that talk to me any kind of way with the expectation that I am going to come back for more. But you have to come back Eliana, Sabrina said, look you missed thanksgiving and we'll let that go, but Christmas is coming up and you are expected to be at the house for dinner on Christmas Eve. While Sabrina was speaking I was thinking to myself, is this for real, one of us has definitely lost our minds, and just in case it's me, Lord hold my tongue because I have already said too much. Look Sabrina, Christmas eve is not looking good for me, my car ran out of gas, I couldn't get my clothes out the cleaners, the sun was in my eyes, I couldn't find my keys, bottom line is don't hold your breath, and don't bet the farm on me being there. You have to be there! She screamed; we are family! Family, I said with my voice raised, family is a condition of the heart Sabrina. Not being born of the same two parents. You don't get to call me family, and mistreat me all in the same five minutes. If this is the definition of family I need to be alone, because my family loves me and wouldn't hurt me. My Pastor is my family, Becky is my family, Sabrina cut me off, I sure hope to see you Christmas Eve, good bye Eliana. And she hung up the phone. I started to pace the floor reviewing my conversation with Sabrina, fuming over the way she talked to me, knowing that she doesn't believe that she said anything wrong. I began to speak out loud, "Lord, I'm not going, I won't be there, I will not deal with this at all. Work with me Lord, help me find my way." Thankful no one was home I laid in my bed reading scriptures until it was time to prepare dinner for Randy.

> Lord, work on my heart, dispel my anger
> Help me to show love and compassion to my family
> Let them see you in me
> Thank you Lord, Amen.

"You have heard that it was said, love you neighbor and hate you enemy. But I tell you; love your enemies and pray for those who persecute you, that you may be sons of your father in heaven. He causes his sun to rise on the evil and the good, and sends rain on the righteous and the unrighteous. If you love those who love you, what reward will you get. Are not even the tax collectors doing that? And if you greet only your brothers, what are you doing more than others? Do not even pagans do that? Be perfect, therefore, as your heavenly father is perfect." (Matthew 5: 43-48)

Christmas came and went without me seeing the McCoy family. I was certain they were angry with me because no one ever called. Separated from all of the people that I spent most of my life with did hurt, but I needed time to deal with all of my feelings. Relationships were broken, words were said, all I knew was I had to find a way to forgive, so that God could forgive me. For the first time in my life I truly felt alone. I learned; watching daddy with his wife and children the importance of family structure and I spent my years building my own family structure, but that too was broken. Once again I sought wisdom from the word of God, and guidance from Pastor Austin.

The one thing that I noticed, not spending time at my parents house was I could focus more on my marriage and my home. Randy and I have always had a very harmonious relationship, but I found us having more arguments lately, not the usual family arguments; like finance or decisions. We were having arguments about trash day being on Thursday, and Randy said he pulled the can out, but it was actually still in the backyard. It was time for us to talk about this.

    I waited until no one was home, and sat Randy down at the kitchen table. "Honey, there is something wrong, something is going on with you, and I don't know what it is, but we need to find out. Randy sat there looking at me and I could tell from his facial expression that he was agitated. Why do you keep saying this Eliana, he responded. There is nothing wrong, nothing is going on with me, I have been having a few headaches, but that's all. Randy, I spoke softly; if you're having headaches we need to go to the doctor to find out what's going on. But this is about more than headaches, you are forgetting things, important things. You're getting lost and turned around when we are out driving. You sometimes say things that don't make any sense. You aren't acting like yourself and I only want to help you. If there is something wrong we should address it now while we can do something about it. What did I just say to you Eliana, I'm not going to see any doctor, he screamed, you are the one that isn't making any sense. I began to cry, Randy I just went through this with daddy, it's true I may be really sensitive about this, but you can't deny the facts, whether or not you want to admit it, something is going on. We made promises to each other to always be up front and brutally honest, if your plan is to back out of that promise then you need to at least tell me that. We are in this together, I will never abandon you Randy nor leave you alone, and I will stay by your side until I take my last breath. Randy let out a deep sigh, no Eliana, Randy dropped his head looking to the floor. I'm not backing out of any promises, I'm just having a difficult time keeping up at work, things that I used to know, now I have to write myself notes, I noticed tears streaming down Randy's face as he continued to speak, I'm having difficulty getting things done and that's making life hard for me right now. I know something is going on; I'm just not ready to do anything about it. I held Randy's hands and looked into his eyes. We have always been in this together, God has propelled our relationship from the very beginning, and nothing will ever change that. I wiped the tears from his face, and kissed him gently on his cheek, I took him by the hand, "Randy you have always been here for me, you had every opportunity to walk away when I became ill, but you didn't; not only did you stand firm by my side, but you helped me with my recovery ever time I've had a relapse, and now it is my turn to be here for you. Not because you did this for me, but because it's what God would have me to do. I pulled Randy up from his chair, Randy, I say now is the time to pray. With everything that has happened Randy was always the one that took us to God in prayer. I thanked God for allowing me an opportunity to help my husband. That night I held Randy in the quiet darkness of our room. I placed his hands on my heart while I prayed.

> Heavenly father, we come before your throne of grace and mercy
> Thanking you, for being God, and loving us as only you can
> We have faced great trials, but you are greater, strengthen us, guide us, speak to our hearts
> We seek you, through your word, may our lives
> Be a display of your divine order
> Bless me Lord to be the helpmeet, which glorifies you, Lord
> Give Randy, the strength and courage to seek what is going on with his body
> Give us wisdom to make the right choices, may everything we do
> Glorify you Lord, in Jesus name, Amen.

As we lay there I stroked Randy's head and whispered, "We're going to be okay, you and me, God has this. No more fighting, we have always come together as one to deal with everything else we have encountered, and this is no different. I only ask that you go to the doctor. Randy whispered; Make me an appointment in the morning. I closed my eyes, thank you Lord.

"Love is patient, love is kind. It does not envy, it does not boast, it is not proud. It is not rude, it is not self-seeking, it is not easily angered, it keeps no record of wrongs. Love does not delight in evil but rejoices with the truth. It always protects, always trusts, always hopes, always perseveres. (1 Corinthians 13: 4-7)

CHAPTER **14**

Never Ending New Beginnings

SO I MADE Randy a doctor's appointment, and waited, since our conversation the arguments ceased. I knew when Randy needed my assistance with something, so I just filled in the gaps for him, and once again harmony was restored to our relationship.

Since daddy's memorial service I hadn't seen or spoken with any of my siblings except that one dreadful conversation with Sabrina, and Easter was quickly approaching. No longer feeling angry, I decided it was time to see my family, the McCoy's. I told my mother we would be attending Easter dinner, and she sounded very excited about it. The closer to Easter, the more unnerved I became. I was filled with anxiety, worried about how they would treat me. I made up my mind, if they were mean to me or any of my family in any way, we were leaving. With that being said, I knew it would be a short visit. We arrived at Tamera's house, and everyone was waiting in the hallway. They were so happy to see us, they took our coats and we hurried into the dining room so we could pray together. The entire day turned out really well, only a few comments, which I was able to ignore, but I didn't want to ruin a good time by staying too long. I approached each family member one on one and expressed my love for them, we got our things and returned home. Maybe we all can just get along. I thought to myself. Things were looking up.

A few days later I awaken from my sleep in pain, my legs were too weak to hold my body up. I couldn't walk without holding on to the walls: I was having a relapse, and needed to go to the hospital. Being familiar with the routine I was once again admitted into the hospital given IV steroids, and started my physical therapy. When I spoke with my doctor I was told that I need to consider a different type of therapy. Unable to take any interferon, I was introduced to a new drug. This new form of therapy was known for having good results in slowing down the progression of multiple sclerosis, however it was also known for causing a brain infection in some patients which resulted in death. I took all the information pamphlets and agreed to make a decision after I researched this thoroughly. Glad to once again be in the comfort of my home I resumed my usual tasks.

While cleaning my telephone rang, it was Raina and Cadence on a conference call. "Cadence is engaged, Raina said sounding very excited. Wow! I'm so very happy for you Cadence, when are you getting married, I asked. I'm not sure later in the year I guess, she responded. Congratulations again Cadence, and I hung up the phone. I thought to myself, maybe things will be different with my family now.

The weekend was approaching and we were expecting Samuel and Phillip over for the weekend. This is it, I thought to myself, when Randy Jr. drop the boys off I will go outside and talk to him. My next thought was, I had absolutely no idea what to say to him. Once again I could hear Randy saying to me, "Eliana, it's time to pray."

> Heavenly father, thank you for this day, this opportunity to be a better example of your love
> Thank you Lord, for your grace and mercy
> Lord, I need to talk to Randy Jr., and I'm not sure what to say
> So I ask you Lord, to guide my heart
> May everything I say be only in love; I seek your divine order
> Your will be done, forgive me Lord, for my shortcomings are many
> I love you Lord, Amen.

Usually when Randy Jr. dropped off the boys he would wait until they entered the house, but this Friday I waited in the door. When he pulled up I walked outside towards his car. After I hugged Samuel and Phillip, I instructed them to go into the house and wait for me at the front door. This was the moment, either he was going to just pull off and drive away or he was going to wait and see what I had to say. Rand put the car in park and got out; I stopped before I reached the car surprised at his actions. Rand walked over to me, hey Rand, I said, hey Eliana, he responded, and I opened my arms to him. Rand walked over to me and we embraced, I was overwhelmed, I had no words to say, I held Rand by his face looking into his eyes, "I miss you Rand that was all I could get out. I miss you too Eliana, he said. I held him as tight as I could, then I started cry, we stood there holding each other while I cried, never saying a word, but thinking, "Thank you Lord, for bringing our son back to us" at this point I knew we would have plenty of opportunities to talk in the future, but right now I needed to express a mother's love without words, unconditional and unadulterated. Looking to the night sky, knowing that once again God answered my prayers I whispered, "Thank you Lord." Before Rand walked away I kissed him and told him I love him. "I love you too Eliana, he said, and he got into his car and drove away. I walked into the house feeling God's restoration working within our relationship. Once I went inside I told Randy what just happened, and he agreed it was time to make things right with his son.

> "Be imtitators of God, therefore, as dearly loved children and live a life of love, just as Christ loved us and gave himself up for us as a fragrant offering and sacrifice to God." (Ephesians 5: 1-2)

Randy's doctor's appointment finally arrived. Randy sat silent while I explained everything that was going on with him. The doctor performed a couple of neurological test, and then decided to order a memory functionality test. Although that bothered me, I knew I couldn't show any emotions in front of Randy. That was one of the first test daddy had before he was diagnosed with Alzheimer's. Although I am hurt about the direction this is going in, we need to know what is going on so we can get the proper help and deal with it.

When we arrived at home Dahlia had some news for us. She was having a baby. Although I wasn't too happy about the circumstance, Dahlia being happy about this was good enough for me. Her pregnancy was quite difficult, and she had a few complications, but the arrival of grandson number five was a wonderful day.

Dahlia went to her doctor's appointment and ended up in the maternity ward having an emergency c-section. I sat in the waiting room waiting for the arrival of our newest edition. When I looked at him my heart felt full of love. There is always joy when a child is born, but when my daughter gave birth to a child, it was more like a personal gift to me from her. I held him in my arms and spoke as I kissed him gently, "hello little one, I'm your Nanna" I looked at the nurses, "What a wonderful miracle from God. Only God can do this." Dahlia named him Alexander and I was completely in love. Because Dahlia had a c-section her hospital stay was longer than expected, but Alexander stayed there with her. I went home to prepare for the homecoming of my daughter and my brand new grandson. The morning she was scheduled to come home from the hospital the telephone rang, it was Dahlia, and she was crying. "Mom, there is something wrong with me! What is it baby, I said trying to remain calm. I need you to come to the hospital." I took a deep breath, every is going to be okay Dahlia, I'll be there in a minute. I called Tamera and asked her to meet me there. I drove to the hospital talking to God the entire way.

> Lord,
> This is my baby, have your way with us
> I don't know what's going on, but I trust you Lord
> Keep me strong, and encouraged Lord, Take care of my babies
>   Lord Dahlia and Alexander
> I love you Lord
> In Jesus name

By the time I arrived at the hospital, they were moving Dahlia into the intensive care unit, the doctors were talking to me, but I couldn't hear everything they were saying. Dahlia had a pulmonary embolism, which is a blockage of the main artery of the lung or one of its branches, by a substance that has traveled from elsewhere in the body through the bloodstream. This is usually fatal if not treated immediately.

Without taking the time to be upset I went into Dahlia's room to be with her. Dahlia looked at me with such pain, not only physical pain, but so much emotional pain, she started to cry, Momma, she said softly, I don't want to leave my baby here. While she was talking the nurses were giving her medication, because they needed her to rest. "Momma, I don't want to close my eyes, I don't want to go to sleep." I stood by Dahlias bedside holding her hand and rubbing her face. As she spoke to me I closed my eyes asking God for composure only he could provide me, "It's okay to go to sleep Dahlia, your body needs the rest you'll be okay." Knowing that only God knows the outcome, but prayerful I continued to speak to my first born child. "You'll be fine, don't worry, the doctors have everything under control, God is not going to take you away from your baby." Please God, I thought to myself, please don't take my baby from me, I don't think I can handle much more. I kissed Dahlia, "I'm right here baby girl and I won't leave your side, I'll check on Alexander in a little while just get some rest." I stayed by Dahlias side until she fell asleep. I walked around to the nursery and checked on Alexander, and then I went into the parking lot to deal with myself. As I approached my car I felt myself let out a scream. It was the only way I could relieve the pressure I was feeling, then I started to cry. "Lord, help me, help my baby, please Lord, give me more time, I was leaning on the car sobbing and talking aloud. Without you Lord I can do nothing, and I need to be strong for my baby and my grandbaby, Lord, give her strength to fight, and guide the doctors, and bless them to give her everything she needs." After thirty minutes in the parking lot it was time to make some phone calls. First I called Dahlia's dad, after I explained to him what was going on his response was to keep him informed. I was infuriated, and promised myself that he would not receive another call from me. Next I called my mom and told her to let everyone know what was going on with Dahlia, and to my surprise no one in my family except Tamera and her son came to the hospital to see Dahlia, not even a phone call. I was hurt for Dahlia, because she has always been a loving child towards each and every one of them. Their lack of attention only confirmed for me that my family is not a priority at all. After speaking to Ray, I can only assume by my tone of voice he could tell he wasn't going to hear from me anymore, because by noon he was there to see Dahlia. I told our children, my friends, and Randy's family and as I expected they were all there at the hospital by the end of the work day. Because only two people were allowed into her room at a time everyone else had to wait in the I.C.U. waiting room. As I sat in my chair Randy held my hand. As I glanced around the room I watched in amazement. Ray and his wife were sitting across from me, he and Randy Jr. were engaged in a conversation, my best friend Haley was talking to Nadia, my God sister Carissa was sitting with her husband William laughing with Randy's niece Laura. The waiting room was full, then I remembered my words to my sister, Family is a condition of the heart, thank you Lord, for blessing me with such a loving family, God has surrounded me with people that love me." I smiled and joined in the many conversations going on while we each waited to spend time with Dahlia. Even under the circumstance it was a party. Recovery for Dahlia was long, but the nurses would bring Alexander around to the unit to spend time with her, and I believe that made all the difference for her. After twelve days Dahlia and baby both came home to start their new lives together.

Lord, thank you
For answering my prayers, not moving my mountains, but taking me over them, what an awesome
God we serve, I love you Lord, Amen.

"Great is our Lord and mighty in power, his understanding has no limit. The lord sustains the humble but casts the wicked to the ground. Sing to the Lord with thanksgiving make music to our God on the harp. He covers the sky with clouds, he supplies the earth with rain and makes grass grow on the hills. He provides food for the cattle and for the young ravens when they call. His pleasure is not in the strength of the horse, nor his delight in the legs of a man; the Lord delights in those who fear him, who put their hope in his unfailing love." (Psalms 147: 5-11)

The day of Randy's test finally arrived, and although he was quite reluctant he did it for me. Afterwards the doctor sat us down in a conference room to discuss the results. They explained that Randy was having some problems with his memory and there were signs of confusion. He was able to perform his usual duties and continue to work for now; he would just need to keep notes as a reminder. Based on his medical history these were signs of dementia, but because of his age they did not want to prescribe any medication, but he would need to consult with his neurologist regularly. Randy and I drove home in silence, and instead of discussing this as we usually did with everything, Randy said he was tired and going to lie down for a nap. I sat alone in the living room with my thoughts. As I sat staring at our family portrait, I began to cry, "Is this what I was being prepared for Lord, I asked looking to the ceiling. I've already had this experience, and there was nothing nice about it. Lord all of the things I saw daddy go through, this is my husband Lord, can I really handle this. Will my health hold up, will I be able to properly provide for Randy everything that he needs, I got down on the floor on my knees and bowed my head, the tears flowing from my eyes creating a puddle on the coffee table, I couldn't see, my voice trembled as I poured out my heart to God.

   Have your way with me Lord, may my vine bear only fruit of
      the spirit

Bless me with courage, understanding, and wisdom
Help me Lord, to deny myself daily, to pick up my cross and follow you
From the rising of the sun, to the going down of the same, I will praise your holy name
Thank you for your gift of love and life
I lift Randy up in prayer, Guide us and allow me to be strong by his side
I ask this prayer in the name of Jesus, Amen.

Although I didn't see my family often, I spoke to my mother regularly; and some of my siblings occasionally. Everyone was a buzz about Cadence's upcoming wedding, and then I found out that my family and I were not invited. By this point in my life I was not surprised, nor disappointed by anything that my family did. I only prayed it wasn't done to hurt me, because the hole that they left in my heart when daddy died was already the size of the Grand Canyon. What did hurt me was Dahlia crying, asking me what she did to deserve this treatment from her family. I couldn't answer her question knowing the only thing she was guilty of was being my child. I told her to pray about it, and let God shine through her heart. In other words, don't hate someone because they hate you; love them in spite of themselves; maybe that will allow God to work on their hearts. I never questioned why I wasn't invited and deep down I guess I didn't care enough to inquire, I only pray that Cadence finds peace and happiness, something which she has always deserved.

In the meantime the changes in Randy were becoming more evident to me and visible to others. Everyday task were beginning to become difficult for him, and everyday he was leaving earlier for work. When I asked him about that, he said he needed more time at work, but I suspected he was having difficulty getting there. I worried about this and prayed for his safety and the safety of others, but Randy was determined to make the best of things, and I continued to pray for patience and understanding so I could provide all the help he needed. I realized I could no longer handle this alone, so I called Randy Jr. and told him what was going on with his dad, and once again sought wisdom from the word of God, and guidance from Pastor Austin.

> "Praise be to the God and father of our Lord Jesus Christ, the father of compassion and the God of all comfort, who comforts us in all our troubles, so that we can comfort those in any trouble with the comfort we ourselves have received from God. For just as the sufferings of Christ flow over into our lives, so also through Christ our comfort overflows. If we are distressed, it is for your comfort and salvation, if we are comforted, it is for your comfort, which produces in you patient endurance of the same sufferings we suffer. And our hope for you is firm, because we know that just as you share in our sufferings, so also you share in our comfort." (2 Corinthians 1: 3-7)

Cadence's wedding came and went, and it was no mistake that we were not invited; I just never knew the reason. I was so preoccupied with my new grandbaby and the joy this new life brought into our household that I didn't "Sweat any of the small stuff."

My nephew Andrew and his wife decided to give my sister Tamera a surprise birthday party, I was reluctant to attend, but decided it would be my final attempt to reach my family. Dahlia and Alexander accompanied Randy and me, and those five hours turned out to be worse than I could have ever imagined. Tamera was her usual self, kind and warm, Wade and Shamar greeted us, Sabrina spoke to me with her back turned as she was talking to Tamera, Cadence said hi as she walked pass me, Raina wouldn't even speak to me although I said hello. They ignored Dahlia and refused to acknowledge Alexander's existence. Every time I entered a room the conversation would cease and everyone would disburse. After a few hours of torture, sitting at a table, I told Randy it was time to leave, I have been treated much worse, by far better people. I made sure, before we left I took a good look at everyone because I knew it was the last time I would see them. As we walked to our vehicle I promised myself, I would never allow them another chance to hurt me or my family again. Too angry to cry, I knew I was madder at myself for putting my family through this, because from past experience I knew better than to expect more from my siblings. A few months later, after Jaclyn started spending time with the family again, she and I had an argument over a barbeque I held at my house, inviting all of my nieces, and nephews without telling her. That was the last time she and I spoke. Although I speak with my mother regularly, she is now the only person that I am in contact with. Although the thought of being without the family that I knew and loved was painful, I know that there is a reason, a season, or a lifetime of people in our lives.

Epilogue

ONCE AGAIN IT was time for thanksgiving, but this year was very different. All of our children were present, and although I could see the change in Randy, I could visibly see God working throughout our household and family. After we gathered in our family circle for prayer we each took turns thanking God, and for the first time I ask Randy Jr. as our eldest child to say the family blessing. What an awesome feeling this was for Randy and I. As we ate dinner together as a family I sat in my chair beside Randy looking around the room at all of our children, and my eyes began to water, the tears started to fall. I closed my eyes, "So this is what daddy felt, when he had his whole family together, I whispered to God." The house was noisy, full of laughter, love and life, "Thank you God, for such a wonderful experience, this is what you mean, to love one another."

After many nights of heartfelt conversations with Raymond, we have found our place with one another, and although Raymond is living in his own apartment he stays with me two weekends a month. He is very helpful when it comes to my care, and our mother son relationship has reached a new level. I still talk with Patrick a couple of times a year and we meet for lunch on occasions. I will allway appreciate his kind words and wisdom, and love him like a father. The more I learn about my family, the more I learn about myself, and I am thankful to each and every one of them, because they helped to shape me into the woman I am today. Although I choose to have no contact with my family I love them, and pray for them daily, knowing God will have his way.

Knowing that there was only more of this to come, I realized through all of the pain and broken-ness I have experience, the loss of my dad, estranged from my birth family, my career as I once knew was over, my health, and Randy's health, I could see God's restoration in my life. I feel as though I was just like the bread from the last supper; God had to take me; out of my comfort zone, removing things I thought was important, but in reality only clouded my focus, then God had to brake me, because I was filled with myself, my own ways, and my desires; The Lord says "Pray without ceasing" I would not have ever developed a prayer life without something to pray about. Through my experiences I have discovered my knees, to surrender myself; to let go and let God have his way, little did I know God would have his way with or without me. Now the Lord can bless me; with my will finally in line with what God wants for me.

> "Then Job replied to the Lord; I know that you can do all things; no plan of yours can be thwarted. You asked, who is that obscures my counsel with knowledge? Surely I spoke of things I did not understand, things too wonderful for me to know. You said listen now, and I will speak; I will question you, and you shall answer me. My ears had heard of you but now my eyes have seen you. Therefore I despise myself and repent in dust and ashes." (Job 42: 1-6)

Heavenly Father
Thank you for the opportunity
To put you first
Thank you Lord
For being such a forgiving God
Thank you
For your love and guidance
Thank you
For never leaving me alone
Thank you Lord
For you promises
Thank you
For loving me in spite of myself
Thank you Lord
For giving me the strength, to pray for my enemies
Thank you Lord
For your grace and mercy
I love you Lord
In Jesus name I pray
Amen

The Serenity Prayer

Lord, grant me the serenity to accept the things I cannot change; the strength to change the things which I can; and the wisdom to know the difference.

CPSIA information can be obtained at www.ICGtesting.com
Printed in the USA
BVOW072129230613

324098BV00001B/99/P